Roger G. Clarke
Analytic Investors

Harindra de Silva, CFA
Analytic Investors

*Steven Thorley, CFA*
*Brigham Young University*

# Fundamentals of
# Futures and Options

RESEARCH FOUNDATION

OF CFA INSTITUTE

## Statement of Purpose

The Research Foundation of CFA Institute is a not-for-profit organization established to promote the development and dissemination of relevant research for investment practitioners worldwide.

ISBN 978-1-934667-63-7

15 November 2013

### Editorial Staff

Elizabeth Collins
Book Editor

Abby Farson Pratt
Assistant Editor

Cindy Maisannes
*Manager*, Publications Production

Randy Carila
Publishing Technology Specialist

# Biographies

**Roger G. Clarke** is chairman of Analytic Investors and also serves as president of a not-for-profit investment organization. Previously, he served on the faculty of Brigham Young University, where he continues to lecture as a guest professor. Dr. Clarke has written numerous articles and papers, including three tutorials for CFA Institute. He has served as a member of the editorial boards of the *Journal of Portfolio Management, Journal of Investment Management*, and *Financial Analysts Journal*. Dr. Clarke received a BA in physics and an MBA from Brigham Young University and an MS in economics and a PhD in finance from Stanford University.

**Harindra de Silva, CFA,** is a portfolio manager at and president of Analytic Investors. He is responsible for the firm's strategic direction and the ongoing development of investment processes. Prior to joining Analytic Investors, Dr. de Silva was a principal at Analysis Group, Inc., where he was responsible for providing economic research services to large institutional investors. He has written many articles and studies on finance-related topics and is an associate editor of the *Financial Analysts Journal*. Dr. de Silva received a BS in mechanical engineering from the University of Manchester Institute of Science and Technology, an MS in economic forecasting and MBA in finance from the University of Rochester, and a PhD in finance from the University of California, Irvine.

**Steven Thorley, CFA,** is the H. Taylor Peery Professor at the Marriott School of Management, Brigham Young University. He is also a consultant for Analytic Investors. Professor Thorley is a member of the investment committees of Deseret Mutual Benefit Administrators, Intermountain Healthcare, and Brigham Young University. He is the author of numerous papers in academic and professional finance journals; he is on the editorial board of the *Financial Analysts Journal* and holds several awards for outstanding research and teaching. Professor Thorley received a BS in mathematics and an MBA from Brigham Young University and a PhD in financial economics from the University of Washington.

# Contents

CE Qualified **CFA Institute**   This publication qualifies for 5 CE credits under the guide-
Activity   lines of the CFA Institute Continuing Education Program.

# Foreword

More than two decades have passed since the Research Foundation of CFA Institute released Roger Clarke's *Options and Futures: A Tutorial*. During this time, the markets for these types of derivatives have grown and matured into highly functional institutions for hedging risk and speculating on price changes of various assets. Granted, there has been a bump or two along the way, most notably surrounding the global financial crisis in 2008 and, before that, the Asian contagion and Long-Term Capital Management crises in the late 1990s. But overall, the global markets for these instruments have functioned quite well.

During this period, the success of options and futures is evidenced by the remarkable increase in the trading volume and the number of different products traded. Although many of these gains have recently moderated, it is difficult to argue with the success when observing from a 20-plus-year perspective.

Still, derivatives are often vilified in the press and by the uninformed—despite their valuable contributions in such areas as helping farmers lock in a price at which they can sell their crops, allowing pension funds to efficiently add to or decrease their equity exposures to manage portfolio risk, and assisting manufacturers in controlling the impact of currency fluctuations on the prices of the goods they buy and sell. Essentially, options and futures help to form a complete market where positions can be taken in practically any attribute of an asset in an efficient manner—a valuable function indeed.

Many changes have occurred in the derivatives markets since Clarke's original work was published. Perhaps two of the largest are (1) electronic trading supplanting open outcry as the platform of choice in a majority of venues and (2) the massive regulatory reforms that have resulted in over-the-counter (OTC) derivatives taking on certain characteristics of exchange-traded products. These two impacts, particularly the changing regulatory environment, are still influencing the markets and will continue to be drivers for change in the future.

Another notable change involves the globalization of derivatives trading. The Asia-Pacific region's share of the global exchange-traded derivatives market has exploded over the past decade, and the region now commands a 36% market share, according to the World Federation of Exchanges. Although the Americas still hold the lead with a 42% market share, the Asia-Pacific region's gains cannot be ignored.

It is within this backdrop of increasing use of derivatives, a wider variety of products trading, more stringent regulation, and expanding globalization that Clarke and his co-authors, Harindra de Silva and Steven Thorley, have produced *Fundamentals of Futures and Options*. The work builds upon the previously released tutorial to provide a valuable updated overview of options and futures.

As executive director of the Research Foundation of CFA Institute and a former options trader, I am honored to present this outstanding book to you. For those of you who are new to options and futures, this work will provide valuable insights into these important investment vehicles. For those of you who have not worked with (or studied) derivatives for a long time, this book will serve as an important review of what was once known but has grown rusty. Through the diligence and hard work of the authors, we now have an updated look at options and futures that can benefit so many of us. We hope you enjoy it.

Bud Haslett, CFA
Executive Director
Research Foundation of CFA Institute

# Acknowledgments

The authors wish to thank Trevor Flint, Spencer Hafen, and James Toone, former MBA research assistants to Professor Thorley, for assistance during this project. We are grateful to the staff at the Research Foundation of CFA Institute, including Laurence B. Siegel, research director, and Walter (Bud) Haslett, CFA, executive director, for their encouragement and support.

# 1. Overview of Derivative Securities and Markets

Although forward agreements for agricultural commodities have been around for centuries, the growth in financial derivatives began in the United States largely in the 1970s with the organization of the Chicago Board Options Exchange (CBOE). Futures on U.S. Treasury bonds and notes began trading in the late 1970s, and options on individual stocks and equity indices began trading in the early 1980s. Since then, not only have derivatives expanded to other countries, but also, the set of underlying indices or assets has expanded tremendously. In many cases, the volume of trading in these instruments now exceeds the volume of trading in physical assets. In addition to the derivatives traded on commodities and currencies, derivatives are now traded on market volatility, inflation, weather, real estate, and a wide array of equity, interest rate, and credit indices. Many of these contracts require complex calculations for modeling the expected payoffs. These calculations could not have been done without the increased data-handling capabilities and computational power of modern computers. Many bright engineers and mathematicians migrated to Wall Street firms to work on the sophisticated models for pricing these complex structures.

In addition to the growth of traditional exchange-traded derivatives, the design of securities with embedded options has become common. Furthermore, many fixed-income transactions that generate an income stream have been dissected and separated into layers of priority in receiving the cash flows. These are sometimes called *structured* or *tranched* securities. In general, the higher-priority tranches have a higher credit quality than the lower-priority tranches. The credit crisis that began in 2007 and 2008 hit these securities particularly hard, and many became worthless.

Swaps are another form of derivatives that have grown substantially since the original edition of this book. Specifically, swaps are used extensively by financial institutions and institutional investors to hedge risk in other assets they hold or to take outright (unhedged) exposures. As with forwards, futures, and options, the volume of trading in the swaps market can exceed the volume of trading in the underlying physical assets. The development of complex derivatives and their expanded use has been an important trend in investment and risk management. We treat only relatively simple option and futures contracts in this book, however, leaving a detailed discussion of more complex derivatives to others. **Table 1.1** shows some of the more popular financial futures contracts as of 2013.

**Table 1.1.   Selected Financial Futures Contracts, Notional Values, and Exchanges**

| Contract | Contract Notional Value | Exchange |
|---|---|---|
| *Equity indices* | | |
| DJIA | $10 × index | CBT |
| Mini DJIA | $5 × index | CBT |
| S&P 500 Index | $250 × index | CME |
| Mini S&P 500 Index | $50 × index | CME |
| Mini Russell 1000 | $100 × index | ICE-US |
| Mini Russell 2000 | $100 × index | ICE-US |
| *Interest rates* | | |
| T-bonds | $100,000 | CBT |
| T-notes | $100,000 | CBT |
| Five-year T-notes | $100,000 | CBT |
| Two-year T-notes | $100,000 | CBT |
| 13-week T-bill | $1,000,000 | CME |
| 30-day federal funds | $5,000,000 | CBT |
| Eurodollar | $1,000,000 | CME |
| *Foreign exchange* | | |
| Japanese yen | ¥12,500,000 | CME |
| British pound | £62,500 | CME |
| Euro | €125,000 | CME |
| Swiss franc | SFr125,000 | CME |
| Canadian dollar | C$100,000 | CME |
| Australian dollar | A$100,000 | CME |

*Notes:* DJIA is Dow Jones Industrial Average; CME is Chicago Mercantile Exchange; CBT is Chicago Board of Trade; and ICE-US is Intercontinental Exchange US.

The growth of derivatives created an incentive for investors to better understand the instruments and the impact they have on asset and risk management. This incentive has manifested itself in several directions.

First, much work has been done by researchers to understand the impact derivatives have on asset management strategies. Institutional investors needed to know how these instruments worked and how they could be used to develop new investment strategies. When the forerunner of this book was first published, the benefits and risks associated with many derivative strategies were not well understood, nor were the processes that were needed when the strategies were implemented. For example, as the size of transactions has increased, an understanding of the cash reserves that need to be set aside for periodic settlement of losses and cross-margining and the management of counterparty exposure has become increasingly important.

Second, the desire for transparency has become much more important than in the past. Specifically, there was not a standard set of rules on how to measure and report derivative security exposures. Analysts could not always tell how much risk an institution had taken on, which made assessing the overall risk profile of the company difficult. Recent rules have brought more standardization to the reporting process, but the issues remain complex and not easily understood by many nonprofessionals.

Third, the growth of derivative transactions and the interconnections between major financial institutions around the world have led to concerns about the integrity of the global financial system. For example, derivatives allow additional leverage to be created in the financial system, and in times of financial turbulence, that leverage can precipitate a liquidity crisis, magnify market moves, and accelerate defaults. These *systemic* concerns have prompted new regulations, new procedures, and new disclosures to increase transparency. For example, the growth of hedge funds that make heavy use of derivatives has drawn the attention of regulators.

## Traditional Derivatives

Option and futures contracts are derivative instruments, which means that they derive their value not from their own intrinsic cash flows or characteristics but from some other underlying security or index. The relationships between the underlying security and its associated option and futures contracts are illustrated in **Figure 1.1**. Note that options may be written on futures contracts, but all option and futures ultimately derive their value from an underlying security or index (one that is *not* an option or futures contract). The links pictured in Figure 1.1 keep the security and its options

**Figure 1.1.   Arbitrage Links**

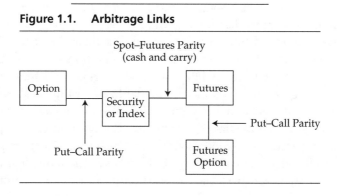

and futures coupled together. The arbitrage link between a futures contract and the underlying security is called *spot–futures parity* or *cash-and-carry arbitrage*. The arbitrage linking put and call options to each other is referred to as *put–call parity*, which, together with spot–futures parity, links the options to the underlying security. Various arbitrage-based relationships and option-pricing models are discussed in more detail in the later chapters of this book.

Futures and option contracts share some common characteristics but also have important differences. The common features of exchange-traded futures and options include standardized contract provisions, trading on organized exchanges, limited maturity, risk management capabilities, and operational efficiencies. The key conceptual difference between futures and option contracts is that a futures position represents the *obligation* to buy (long position) or sell (short position) the underlying asset in the future whereas an option represents the *right*, but not the obligation, to buy (call option) or sell (put option) the underlying asset in the future.

Simply put, a futures contract is an agreement between a buyer and a seller to trade an underlying security or index at a future date. The most popular futures contracts are traded on organized exchanges and have standardized contracts specifying how much of the security is to be bought or sold, when the transaction will take place, what features the underlying security must have, and how delivery or transfer of the security is to be handled. To encourage futures contract buyers and sellers to follow through with the transaction, a good faith deposit, called *initial margin*, is required from both parties when a contract is initiated.

As the price of the underlying security changes from day to day, the price of the futures contract also changes. The buyer and seller of exchange-traded futures contracts recognize this daily gain or loss by transferring cash to the margin account of the party reaping the benefit. This *mark-to-market* practice keeps large unrealized losses from accumulating and reduces the probability of one of the parties defaulting on the obligation.

Option contracts possess some of these same features, but the buyer of an option contract has limited liability and can lose, at most, the price paid for the option, sometimes called the option's *premium*. But the seller of the option has unlimited liability, which is similar to the parties to a futures contract. As a result, the option seller is usually required to post initial margin, as in a futures contract.

The exchange-traded contracts' standardized features allow futures and options to be traded quickly and efficiently on organized exchanges. Exchanges serve as intermediaries to facilitate trading, transfer daily gains and losses between parties, and pool resources of exchange members to guarantee financial stability if a single investor should default. The individual parties to a given trade may never meet and do not need to deal with each other after the exchange has matched their trade. The exchange's clearinghouse function allows buyers or sellers to reverse a position before maturity and thus close out the obligation without having to find the party that initially took the other side of the trade. For example, a previous buyer of a futures contract merely sells a contract with the same parameters, and the clearinghouse cancels the buyer's original obligation. In fact, although the buyer of selected futures contracts can require delivery of the underlying assets on the expiration date, most positions are canceled prior to expiration, so actual delivery is uncommon. The highest volume of trading, and thus the most liquidity, usually occurs in the contracts with the nearest maturity dates. As the expiration date of the near-term contract approaches, investors who want to maintain a futures position simply reverse their position in the nearest-term contract and roll their exposure over to the next nearest-term contract.

In addition to the exchange-traded securities that are the focus of this book, there are other types of derivatives contracts, such as forwards and swaps. They have characteristics similar to those of exchange-traded futures and options but are contracts between two specific parties and are referred to as *over-the-counter* (OTC) contracts. Settlement of gains and losses on OTC contracts are not guaranteed by a central clearing organization, so each side of the transition has counterparty risk exposure. In periods of financial stress, there may be heightened concern over the ability of a counterparty to settle outstanding claims, which introduces an additional element of risk. To reduce the risk that a counterparty may not be able to settle any losses at the expiration of the OTC contract, counterparties have recently been requiring marking to market of any losses along the way, similar to the daily mark-to-market process for exchange-traded derivatives.

The use of options and futures gives the investor flexibility in managing the risk of an underlying security or index. Basic business activities, such as banking, international trading, and providing retirement benefits, may leave an individual investor or corporation exposed to interest rate, foreign exchange, or equity market risk. The use of options and futures allows the investor to hedge or transfer all or some of this risk to others more willing to bear it. Derivative securities can also be used in a speculative way, although most applications in this tutorial concern risk control or the risk-hedging aspect of futures and option trading. We focus on contracts for financial assets, such as stocks, bonds, and foreign exchange, but structured derivative contracts exist for metals, energy, agricultural commodities, and other physical commodities.

Trading in options and futures contracts has some operational advantages, in addition to risk management, over trading in the underlying securities:

- easy adjustment of market exposure,

- reduced transaction costs,

- same-day settlement of simultaneous trades,

- less disruption of underlying asset management, and

- creation of specialized risk/return patterns.

The use of futures and option contracts allows broad market exposure to be adjusted at low transaction costs. In addition, unlike the trades in many underlying securities, derivative securities have same-day settlement. Furthermore, positions in derivative securities can be initiated without the need to buy or sell the underlying securities, which produces less disruption to an existing investment program. Finally, derivative securities can be used to create specialized return patterns.

The use of futures and option contracts also has some disadvantages:

- the need to understand complex relationships,

- potential tracking error against the underlying security or index,

- requirement of liquidity reserves to post and meet margin requirements,

- daily settlement associated with marking to market, and

- potential short-term tax consequences.

Some investors may lack the understanding and experience to use futures and options effectively. The specifications within futures and option contracts may not exactly match the investor's portfolio, and derivative contracts can become slightly mispriced with respect to the underlying asset, both of which lead to tracking error in the investor's strategy. Derivative securities can require more attention than other securities do because of the daily mark-to-market aspect and the need to maintain cash reserves. Finally, futures and options have relatively short lives, and closing out positions often creates special considerations for taxable investors.

## Recent Innovations

The largest and most important derivative category *not* covered in this book is the swap market, wherein investors effectively trade one income stream for another. A swap represents a complex combination of futures contracts. Although swaps are beyond the scope of this book, four other derivative structures that have been more recently introduced to the marketplace are briefly reviewed here: volatility, credit, real estate, and weather contracts.

Starting in the mid-1990s, trading derivatives based on equity market volatility became popular. Volatility derivatives gain or lose value depending on how the volatility of the equity market changes, not on the level of the market itself. Prominent derivatives in this category include variance swaps and futures or options written on a volatility index, such as CBOE Market Volatility Index (VIX). Investors have found that volatility derivatives are useful for hedging equity risk because a long volatility position typically exhibits a strong negative correlation with sizable movements in the equity market. Specifically, volatility tends to increase when the market drops sharply and then subside as the market recovers. But the effectiveness of volatility derivatives as a hedge is based on a general tendency because the payoff is driven by the change in market volatility, not the direction of the market move itself, in contrast to the simple futures contracts that we will cover later in detail.

Credit default swaps (CDS) became some of the most popular—and then most infamous—financial derivatives traded. Contracts have been constructed both on portfolios of separate underlying credits and on individual corporate names. The buyer of a CDS pays a premium, or fee, to the seller of the swap. In the case of a credit event, the seller makes a cash payment back to the buyer. Credit events are typically defined as some form of bankruptcy, failure to pay, restructuring, repudiation, moratorium, obligation default, or obligation acceleration. The basic intent of credit derivatives is to transfer credit risk from lenders to third parties while retaining ownership of the asset. A CDS may thus be regarded as a form of insurance contract, insuring the buyer against credit default and other negative events, although "true" insurance involves pooling of risks and a CDS does not.

Property derivatives derive their value from underlying real estate assets. Property derivatives are usually tied to a real estate property index, not to a specific property. The most common forms are a total return swap, a forward contract, and a futures contract on an index. The buyer of the derivative receives a payment from the seller if the property index increases and pays the seller if the property index decreases during the term of the contract. The two most popular real estate indices in the United States are Radar Logic's RPX and the S&P/Case–Shiller Home Price Index. Property derivatives allow the investor to gain or reduce exposure to the property market, either as a hedge against physical assets or as a pure investment position, without having to transact in the underlying properties themselves.

Weather derivatives can be used to take positions with respect to adverse or unexpected weather conditions. For example, one of the most common units of measure in weather derivatives is heating degree days (HDD). Contracts based on HDD are currently traded for about 25 cities in the United States. These contracts can help businesses hedge unexpected energy costs of heating or cooling buildings on the basis of changes in temperature measured in specific locations. Other weather contracts are based on the amount of precipitation (rain or snow) in a particular location. Additional derivatives are tied to the scale of damage from hurricanes or earthquakes. If damages exceed a certain amount, one party helps cover the cost of the damages incurred by the other. These derivatives became popular in the mid-1990s as insurance companies looked for ways to spread the risk of insuring the damages from catastrophic events. These types of derivatives also provide an interesting alternative whose returns are uncorrelated with the returns from typical financial markets. The creation of new derivative contracts that meet the risk transfer and speculative needs of various investors will undoubtedly continue in the 21st century, as will the development of regulatory structures to ensure well-functioning financial markets.

# 2. Futures Contracts: Pricing Relationships

A futures contract provides an opportunity to commit now to purchase or sell an underlying asset at a specified price, with delivery and payment delayed until the settlement date. A futures contract can be either "bought" or "sold." The buyer of a futures contract has a *long position* and commits to buying the underlying asset or security at the specified price and date. No money changes hands up front, except for the posting of initial margin. The seller of a futures contract has a *short position* and commits to selling the underlying asset or security at the specified price and date. The fact that the futures price is negotiated now but delivery and payment are delayed until the settlement date creates an opportunity cost for the seller in receiving payment. As a result, the negotiated price for future delivery of the asset differs from the current cash price by an amount that reflects the cost of waiting to get paid.

Strictly speaking, a two-party buy/sell agreement without margin requirements or a mark-to-market feature is simply forward contracting, which was a common practice for trading agricultural commodities (e.g., wheat) long before the establishment of formal futures exchanges in the 20th century. The more formal futures contract contains many of the same elements as a forward agreement, but gains or losses that accrue as the price of the underlying asset fluctuates are realized on a day-to-day basis. In other words, the total accumulated gain or loss is the same for a futures contract as for a forward agreement but is realized (cash is transferred) on a daily basis instead of on the final settlement date. Futures contracts also require the posting of initial margin or a performance bond with the broker to initiate the trade. In recent years, some counterparties in forward agreements have required settlement of interim gains and losses if they exceed some predetermined amount. In either case, the purpose of posted margin is to reduce the chance that one of the parties to the trade builds up substantial losses and then defaults. The minimum size of the initial margin varies for different futures contracts but usually amounts to between 2% and 10% of the notional contract value, as set by the exchange where the contract is traded. Contracts on more volatile securities or indices generally require higher percentage margins than contracts on less volatile securities or indices and are occasionally adjusted by the exchanges in response to market conditions.

Another difference between forward agreements and futures contracts is that futures contracts have standardized provisions specifying maturity date and contract size, so they can be traded on organized exchanges. Most actively traded markets use futures contracts, although a substantial forward market for foreign exchange exists through the banking system. In the United States, the futures markets are regulated by the Commodity Futures Trading Commission, but individualized forward agreements are not. In this book, we will generally treat futures as forward agreements in discussing pricing relationships and risk management properties. If interest rates are constant and the term structure is flat, the two will theoretically be priced the same. Although these interest rate conditions are not strictly met in practice, the difference in price between a futures contract and a forward agreement is usually small.

Where do futures come from? Ordinarily, we think of securities as being issued (sold for the first time) by organizations wanting capital. Such organizations are typically corporations or governments. Futures, however, are created through the exchanges when one investor commits to purchase a security at a specified date from an investor who commits to sell. No new underlying security is created in the process, only a commitment to exchange at the specified future date.

**Table 2.1** lays out some of the algebraic notation we will use in referring to futures contracts. At Time 0, or "now," the underlying security and each of two futures contracts has a current price, subscripted by 0. Remember that the futures price is the price investors agree on today for delayed purchase or sale of the security at a future expiration date. Futures contracts are usually traded with several different expiration dates, although for simplicity, Table 2.1 includes contracts for only two dates—a nearby date, Time 1, and a "deferred" date, Time 2—as shown by superscripts. When the first of these two dates arrives, the underlying security price will probably have moved to a new value, subscripted by 1. The change in the price of the underlying security also leads to new prices for both futures contracts, also subscripted by 1. When the second date arrives, the security price will have moved again to yet another new value, subscripted by 2. Note that after Time 1 has passed, the nearby futures contract has expired and is no longer traded, so no price is listed for Time 2.

As our first example of the Time 0 prices in Table 2.1, we quote in **Table 2.2** the futures prices for the Mini S&P 500 contract for the close of markets on Tuesday, 15 May 2012. The S&P 500 Index closed that day at 1,330.66. As shown in Table 2.2, the June futures contract price is a bit lower, at

**Table 2.1.   Algebraic Notation for Futures Prices**

| Price | Time 0 (now) | Time 1 | Time 2 |
|---|---|---|---|
| Security price | $S_0$ | $S_1$ | $S_2$ |
| Nearby futures price | $F_0^1$ | $F_1^1$ | — |
| Deferred futures price | $F_0^2$ | $F_1^2$ | $F_2^2$ |

**Table 2.2.  Futures Prices for Mini S&P 500 Contracts on Tuesday, 15 May 2012**

|  | Settlement Price | Open Interest |
|---|---|---|
| Index | 1,330.66 |  |
| June settlement | 1,328.25 | 2,870,892 |
| September settlement | 1,321.75 | 32,285 |

1,328.25, and the September futures price is lower still, at 1,321.75. As the reader will see, the arbitrage pricing relationship causes the contract with the more distant expiration date to have a lower price because the dividend yield on U.S. stocks is currently greater than the interest opportunity cost of money (i.e., prevailing short-term U.S. interest rates).

In some prior periods (say, the 1990s), prevailing short-term interest rates were higher than the dividend yield on stocks, so futures prices were increasingly higher for more distant expiration dates. If short-term interest rates move higher than dividend yields in future years, then the pattern of futures prices will shift back to being increasingly higher for more distant expiration dates.

The last column of Table 2.2 gives the open interest, defined as the number of contracts that have been purchased and are still outstanding. The specification for each Mini S&P 500 futures contract is $50 multiplied by the index level (see Table 1.1), so the notional value of each June contract is $50 × 1,330.66 = $66,533.00. Although no "price" is paid now for a short or long position in the futures contract, the initial margin requirement set by the exchange might be $5,625 per contract. Notice that most of the open interest shown in Table 2.2 is in the nearby June contract rather than the September contract.

The data in Table 2.2 can be used to illustrate the mark-to-market response to daily fluctuations in the futures price. Suppose that on Wednesday, 16 May 2012, the June futures contract drops 6.00 points. The price move generates a loss of $50 × 6.00 = $300 per contract, which is taken out of the margin account for the long position (i.e., the prior buyer of this futures contract) and placed in the margin account for the short position (i.e., a prior seller of this contract). Over time, the mark-to-market transferring of cash from one investor's margin account to another's account will be the same as if the cash transfers were all postponed to the expiration date, as they might be in a simple forward agreement.

Also notice the implicit leverage involved in buying or selling a futures contract. For a 6-point drop in the June futures price, the percentage change is only 6.00/1,330.66 = 0.45%. The margin account of investors with a short position in the June futures increases by $300 per contract, a gain of 300/5,625 = 5.33% on the initial margin deposited and a leverage factor of about 11.8 to 1 (5.33/0.45). So, futures can be used in a highly leveraged way or a conservative way, depending on how much the investor commits to the initial margin account. The leverage factor in this example is 11.8 to 1.0 because the initial margin requirement of \$5,625 is 8.45% of the \$66,533.00 notional value and 11.8 is the reciprocal of 8.45%. If the investor had posted a larger initial margin of 20%, or $0.20 \times \$66,533.00 = \$13,306.60$, the leverage factor would be only 5 to 1 because 5 is the reciprocal of 20%. If the investor chose to put the full dollar equivalent of the notional futures index, \$66,533.00, into the margin account, there would no leverage effect at all; in other words, the leverage factor would be 1 to 1.

## Pricing a Generic Futures Contract

As mentioned in the specific example for the Mini S&P 500 futures contract, the futures price is related to the price of the underlying security or asset, the opportunity cost until expiration, and any expected cash distributions by the underlying asset before expiration. Note that futures are priced in an open market, where the orders of many buyers and sellers are matched like any other financial asset, but the futures contract *price* is tied to the price of the underlying security or index because of the cash-and-carry arbitrage condition. When the underlying asset price changes, the price of the futures contract will also change in order to maintain the link. The cash-and-carry arbitrage argument for a simple futures contract (ignoring mark-to-market effects) is as follows: Suppose an underlying security with a current price $S_0$ is scheduled to pay a cash flow distribution of $CF_t$ at time $t$. ($CF_t$ might be a dividend or bond coupon payment.) **Table 2.3** outlines two investment strategies that each result in holding the security at time $t$, right after the cash distribution has been paid. In Strategy I, the investor simply buys the underlying security, ending up with $S_t + CF_t$ at time $t$. In Strategy II, the investor establishes a long futures position and saves the funds that would have been used to purchase the security in an account earning an annualized interest rate, $r$. At time $t$, the investor has accumulated $S_0(1+r)^t$ in the savings account and buys the underlying security for the agreed futures price of $F_0$, independent of its actual ending value, $S_t$.

**Table 2.3.   Cash-and-Carry Arbitrage**

| | Value at Time 0 | Value at Time $t$ |
|---|---|---|
| Strategy I: Purchase the security | $S_0$ | $S_t + CF_t$ |
| Strategy II: | | |
| Invest $S_0$ dollars at rate $r$ for time $t$ | $S_0$ | $S_0(1+r)^t$ |
| Establish a long futures position | 0 | $S_t - F_0$ |
| Total value for Strategy II | $S_0$ | $S_0(1+r)^t + S_t - F_0$ |

Because both strategies begin with the same dollar investment and both end up owning the security at time $t$, the ending values should also be equal. In other words, the value of Strategy I at time $t$ should equal the value of Strategy II at time $t$:

$$S_t + CF_t = S_0 (1+r)^t + S_t - F_0. \tag{2.1}$$

Solving for the futures contract price established at Time 0 gives the arbitrage-free, or "fair," futures price as

$$F_0 = S_0 (1+r)^t - CF_t. \tag{2.2}$$

Thus, the futures contract price represents the current price of the security adjusted for the opportunity cost of delayed settlement. The seller of the security is compensated for waiting to receive the money by implicitly earning interest on the current value of the security, netted against any cash distributions paid on the underlying security before settlement. The adjustment of the underlying security price to arrive at the futures price is sometimes referred to as the *cost of carry*. Notably, the current futures price does not represent the expected price of the underlying security at the expiration date. Whatever investor expectations are, they will be embodied in the current security price and affect the current futures price through the arbitrage link.

Alternatively, for a quoted futures price, $F_0$, and any scheduled cash flows, $CF_t$, one can use this relationship to infer what interest rate the buyer has to pay to compensate the seller, which is referred to as the *implied repurchase rate* (or simply, *repo rate*). In most cases, the market adjusts the futures price until the repo rate equals a widely available short-term interest rate, such as the Treasury bill yield rate or London Interbank Offered Rate (LIBOR). If the implied repo rate is substantially higher or lower than these market rates, arbitrageurs could create a riskless position to capture the differential return. Specifically, a riskless return higher than the short-term interest rate could be earned by selling an overvalued futures contract and buying the security. Alternatively, funds could be borrowed at below-market rates by buying an undervalued futures contract and selling the security.

To illustrate how the arbitrage works if the repo rate implied by the futures price is too high, consider the following numerical example. A $100 security is scheduled to pay $2 in one month, with the futures price trading at a value of $99, which is too low. Specifically, an investor with a short futures position could buy the security today at $100 and sell it in one month at the contracted price of $99—regardless of what the market price of the security ends up being at that time. The one-month percentage return, including the $2 cash distribution, is (99 + 2)/100 − 1 = 1%, or a simple annualized return of 12%. Thus, market participants would be enticed to sell the futures contract and purchase the security until their relative prices adjusted enough to result in a rate of return more consistent with market interest rates, which are currently much less than 12%. The reverse will happen (i.e., market participants will buy futures contracts and short the underlying asset) if the repo rate implied by the futures price is too low (i.e., the futures price is too high).[1]

We now modify the generic cash-and-carry arbitrage formula to accommodate four specific underlying assets: equity index futures, T-bond futures, Eurodollars, and currency futures. Again, we will disregard any complications from marking to market, so the futures contract will behave like a forward contract.

## Equity Index Futures Pricing

If the underlying security is an equity index that pays periodic dividends, then the generic formula in Equation 2.2 need only be modified in terms of notation, with $D_t$ for a dividend at time $t$ replacing the more generic $CF_t$ for cash flow at time $t$:

$$F_0 = S_0(1+r)^t - D_t. \qquad (2.3)$$

Thus, when equity dividend yields are greater than short-term interest rates, as is the case at the writing of this book, the fair futures price will be less than the underlying index. This situation can be seen more clearly by modifying Equation 2.3 to incorporate the annualized dividend yield, $d$, expressed as a yield on the initial price:

$$F_0 = S_0(1+r-d)^t. \qquad (2.4)$$

Equation 2.4 makes it clear that if $d > r$, then $F_0 < S_0$ for any positive length of time $t$. If short-term interest rates revert to levels higher than equity dividend yields, as they were for most of the latter half of the 20th century, then $r > d$ and the futures price will again exceed the current index value, $F_0 > S_0$.

Consider, as an example, the Mini S&P 500 contract in which the two closest quarterly expiration dates are June and September, shown in Table 2.2. Note that this futures contract does not require the actual purchase or sale of the shares of stock at the expiration date; it "settles in cash." In other words, if held to expiration, the contract is settled as a cash payment equivalent to the difference between the index value at that date, $S_t$, and the futures price established up front, $F_0$. Specifically, the long futures position receives a cash flow of $S_t - F_0$ through the settlement process at the exchange. If $S_t - F_0$ turns

---

[1]In contrast to financial futures, shorting the underlying asset may be difficult for some commodities, which can create an asymmetry in the arbitrage condition. Imagine taking a short position in sheep; to get started, you would have to borrow the sheep! In these instances, the futures price is rarely higher than its arbitrage value, but it can sometimes go below its arbitrage value because the reverse arbitrage of buying the futures contract and shorting the commodity may be difficult to execute.

out to be negative, then the holder of the long position pays the exchange, which then settles with the holder of a short position.

As of the date of this example, 15 May 2012, the *Wall Street Journal* quoted a short-term interest rate as 0.24% per year. On the same date, the annual dividend yield on S&P 500 stocks was quoted as 2.09%. The nearby contract in Table 2.2 expires on 15 June 2012, exactly one month from the quote date of 15 May. Given that the current (15 May) level of the S&P 500 is 1,330.66, the fair price of the June futures contract, according to the arbitrage-free formula in Equation 2.4, would be

$$F_0 = 1{,}330.66(1 + 0.0024 - 0.0209)^{1/12} = 1{,}328.59,$$

which is close to the actual quote of 1,328.25. This mispricing is probably not large enough to take advantage of in terms of an arbitrage trade after transaction costs are taken into account.

Suppose, however, that the futures price were quoted at 1,330.25. Then, solving for $r$ in the arbitrage-free formula of Equation 2.4 would give the annualized repo rate as

$$\left(\frac{1{,}330.25}{1{,}330.66}\right)^{12} - 1 + 2.09\% = 1.72\%,$$

which might signal an exploitable arbitrage opportunity at current interest rates. Specifically, if the futures contract price were set at 1,330.25, a large institutional investor could borrow U.S. dollars for one month at the annualized rate of 0.24% and set up a risk-free return of 1.72%.

## Bond Futures Pricing

At its core, the pricing of a bond futures contract is driven by the same arbitrage principle as any other financial futures contract. Specifically, the arbitrage-free futures price is equal to the current bond price adjusted for delayed delivery by using a short-term interest rate minus any interim cash flows. Several bond market and bond futures contract conventions, however, complicate a simple demonstration of arbitrage trades. These complications include flexibility in what constitutes the underlying asset, the quoting conventions of "accrued interest," and nondecimal pricing.

The first complication to the arbitrage logic for bond futures is that the underlying asset that drives the arbitrage may be one of several different bond issues. For example, the T-note futures contract listed under "Interest rates" in Table 1.1 can be satisfied with delivery of almost any U.S. Treasury security with a maturity from 6.5 to 10.0 years and a variety of coupons. Thus, calculation of the fair futures price must include a factor that converts the price of any particular bond to one common standard, generally described as the "10-year 6% coupon bond."

The second complicating issue is that bond price quotes include an accrued interest factor that adjusts the actual trading price for the days before the next semiannual coupon payment. Finally, bond prices are almost always quoted as a percentage of par value (instead of, say, dollars, euros, or yen), which in and of itself is not a problem. But for increments in price finer than a whole percent, bond markets often use 32nds of a percent rather than decimals.

**Table 2.4** shows futures prices for the T-note contract trading on the Chicago Mercantile Exchange (CME) on 15 May 2012 for both June (one month out) and September (four months out) settlements. The June contract has a price of 133-12, or 133 and 12/32nds of a percent of $1,000. After some arithmetic, the price works out to be $1,333.75 established today (15 May 2012) for delivery of an allowable T-note one month from now. In the second example in Table 2.4, the September futures price of 132-11 is 132 and 11/32nds of a percent of $1,000, which translates into $1,323.44 after rounding to the nearest cent.

Note that the pattern in Table 2.4 of declining prices for longer settlement contracts is the same as it was for equity index futures in Table 2.2. The pattern is driven by the fact that in 2012, short-term interest rates were lower than the coupon rates underlying the futures contract prices. If short-term interest rates were to move to higher levels at some future date, then the T-note futures contract prices would increase with longer settlement dates. Also, actual delivery in settlement of a single contract requires 100 bonds. U.S. Treasury bonds have par values of $1,000 per bond, so the notional value of one T-note futures contract is $100,000, as shown in Table 1.1.

Including a factor, $f$, for conversion to the standard "10-year 6% coupon" bond price and accrued interest adjustment, $AI$, renders the generic cost-of-carry arbitrage formula for futures in Equation 2.2 for bonds as

$$F_0 = \frac{(S_0 + AI)(1+r)^t}{f}. \tag{2.5}$$

Although a 10-year 6% coupon Treasury was not in the market on 15 May 2012, there was a newly issued 1.75% coupon bond with a maturity date of 15 May 2022 expiring in exactly 10 years. The price quote for that bond on 15 May was 99 25/32% of par, or $997.81, which constitutes a yield to maturity of

**Table 2.4. Futures Prices for T-Note Contracts on Tuesday, 15 May 2012**

| Settlement Month | Settlement Price | Open Interest |
|---|---|---|
| June | 133-12 | 1,854,934 |
| September | 132-11 | 20,190 |

1.77%. An investor with an outstanding short position in the June futures contract could choose to settle that contract by delivering the 1.75% coupon bond but would have to apply an issue-specific conversion factor. Conceptually, the conversion factor would be calculated as the price at which the 1.75% coupon bond would have a 6.00% yield. For example, ignoring the fact that the bond would be just shy of a full 10-year maturity in June 2012, a simple bond calculation (exact 10-year maturity and 20 semiannual coupon payments of 0.875% to yield 3.000%) gives a conversion factor of 0.6839. In fact, the official conversion factor posted by the CME for this bond as settlement of the June futures contract was slightly higher at 0.6897. The conversion factor for this same 1.75% bond for the September, rather than June, futures contract was 0.6956.

Because the futures contract allows many different bonds to be delivered in settlement of the contract, the price is generally driven by the "cheapest-to-deliver" bond, which may not be the 1.75% coupon bond. Thus, we cannot directly verify the cost-of-carry formula, Equation 2.5, using the 1.75% coupon bond, even given the conversion factor. Specifically, the 1.75% bond is not likely to be the cheapest-to-deliver bond, so a direct application of Equation 2.5 would result in an implied repo rate that would have been materially below prevailing short-term interest rates, perhaps even negative. The implied repo rate would be biased low because the cheapest-to-deliver bond (found by a search over all admissible bonds for the lowest value of $S_0/f$, with accrued interest ignored) would, by definition, result in a higher $r$.

However, we can use the conversion factors for the newly issued 1.75% coupon bond to determine the *relative* fairness of the *two* futures quotes in Table 2.4. The spot price, $S_0$, and accrued interest, $AI$, fall out, and the cost-of-carry arbitrage *between* the futures contracts is

$$\frac{f_2 F_0^2}{f_1 F_0^1} = (1+r)^{t_2-t_1}, \tag{2.6}$$

where $F_0^1$ and $F_0^2$ are the current (15 May 2012) futures prices of, respectively, the near-term (June) and longer-term (September) contracts; $f_1$ and $f_2$ are the conversion factors for any specific deliverable bond; and $t_2 - t_1$ is the time, in years, between contract settlement dates. Given the prices quoted in Table 2.4 and the conversion factors for the newly issued 1.75% coupon bond, Equation 2.6 produces

$$\frac{0.6956(1,323.44)}{0.6897(1,333.75)} = (1+r)^{3/12},$$

which implies an annualized repo rate of $r = 0.30\%$, close to the level of short-term interest rates in May 2012. To be precise, the implied repo rate in this calculation represents the *forward* interest rate for the three months from 15

June to 15 September, rather than the one-month *spot* rate on 15 May. See the appendix for a discussion of forward rates and spot rates.

## Eurodollar Futures Pricing

Eurodollar futures, perhaps the most widely traded contracts in the world, are listed as the last item under "Interest rates" in Table 1.1. Eurodollar contracts are cash settled, but the underlying asset is the three-month interest rate on U.S. dollar deposits established in Europe. The contracts have a notional value of $1,000,000 and, like the other futures contracts we have discussed, quarterly expiration dates.

For example, **Table 2.5** provides quotes for June and September Eurodollar futures on 15 May 2012.

Eurodollar futures are quoted as an index formed by subtracting the percentage forward rate for the three-month LIBOR from 100. Arbitrage-free pricing may not be as apparent in Eurodollar futures as in the other contracts we have studied, but the arbitrage process does keep these settlement prices consistent with implied forward rates.

**Table 2.5. Futures Prices for Eurodollars on Tuesday, 15 May 2012**

| Settlement Month | Settlement Price | Open Interest |
|---|---|---|
| June | 99.495 | 960,070 |
| September | 99.375 | 934,289 |

## Currency Futures Pricing

The fair pricing of a futures contract on foreign exchange follows the same basic arbitrage logic of the other futures contracts. Specifically, the futures price is equal to the spot currency exchange rate adjusted for the relative cost of funds in each of the two currencies:

$$F_0 = S_0 \left( \frac{1+r_d}{1+r_f} \right)^t,$$

(2.7)

where

$r_d$ = short-term domestic interest rate

$r_f$ = short-term foreign interest rate

$S_0$ = current exchange rate (quoted as home currency per foreign currency)

Equation 2.7 incorporates an opportunity cost at the domestic interest rate as well as the opportunity cost at the foreign interest rate. Because it involves two separate interest rates, this arbitrage relationship is often called *covered interest arbitrage*.

To understand covered interest arbitrage, consider the two following invest-ments. In one strategy, the investor saves $1.00 (the domestic currency in this example) at an annual rate of $r_d$ for $t$ years. As an alternative strategy, the inves-tor could convert $1.00 to the foreign currency (i.e., divide by the exchange rate, $S_0$), receive interest at the foreign rate, $r_f$, for $t$ years, and contract to convert the proceeds back into the domestic currency at the forward exchange rate, $F_0$.

Because both strategies invest the same beginning amount and result in the accumulation of a known amount at expiration, both strategies should result in the same value at time $t$. In other words,

$$\$1.00\,(1+r_d)^t = \frac{\$1.00}{S_0}(1+r_f)^t F_0.$$

Solving for the appropriate forward exchange rate, $F_0$, gives the expression for the covered interest arbitrage in Equation 2.7.

For a numerical example, consider the currency futures contract between U.S. and Australian dollars, listed as the last item in Table 1.1. The spot exchange rate in USD/AUD terms is 0.9936, so that an Australian dollar is worth 99.36 U.S. cents. **Table 2.6** shows the futures contract prices for June and September settlement of USD/AUD exchange rates. The open interest is substantially higher for the near-term contract, as is typical for most futures. The futures price is lower for the deferred expira-tion in Table 2.6 because the interest rate in Australian dollars is higher than the U.S. dollar interest rate. For example, three-month Australian Treasury bills were priced to yield an annualized 3.20% on 15 May; corre-sponding three-month U.S. Treasury bills were priced to yield an annual-ized rate of only 0.07%.

**Table 2.6. Futures Prices for Australian Exchange Rates on Tuesday, 15 May 2012**

|  | Settlement Price | Open Interest |
|---|---|---|
| Spot price | 0.9936 | |
| June settlement | 0.9915 | 144,207 |
| September settlement | 0.9834 | 650 |

To check on the fairness of the futures prices in Table 2.6, we can apply the covered interest arbitrage formula using the current exchange rate and the respective interest rates of the two currencies. For example, the arbitrage-free futures price for June settlement is

$$F_0 = 0.9936\left(\frac{1+0.0007}{1+0.0320}\right)^{1/12} = 0.9911,$$

which is quite close to the June futures quote of 0.9915 in Table 2.6. Similarly, the arbitrage-free futures price for September settlement,

$$F_0 = 0.9936\left(\frac{1 + 0.0007}{1 + 0.0320}\right)^{4/12} = 0.9835,$$

is also quite close to the 0.9834 quote in Table 2.6.

As with contracts on other types of financial assets, the fair futures price does not represent the price that investors forecast for the underlying asset in the future. Those expectations are captured in the current spot price and influence the futures price only indirectly through the arbitrage relationship. The futures price is simply the price for delayed settlement of the transaction.

## Basis and Calendar Spread Relationships

The difference between the spot price of the underlying asset and the futures price, $S_0 - F_0$, is often referred to as the contract's *basis*. Using the cash-and-carry logic on an underlying security with expected cash flow $CF_t$, we find the arbitrage-free basis should be

$$\text{Basis} = S_0 - F_0 = S_0\left[1 - (1 + r)^t\right] + CF_t. \tag{2.8}$$

Because the expected cash flows from the underlying asset often exceed the opportunity cost of funds, the basis is often positive. For an underlying asset with zero expected cash flow, however, the basis defined as $S_0 - F_0$ would be negative. In that case, for convenience, analysts commonly reverse the definition of the basis to $F_0 - S_0$ so that it is a positive number. Specifically, for an underlying asset with zero cash flows, the fair basis is often quoted as

$$\text{Basis} = F_0 - S_0 = S_0\left[(1 + r)^t - 1\right]. \tag{2.9}$$

For either definition of the basis, the interest opportunity cost of funds, as well as any expected cash flows, declines as the futures expiration date nears. This decline forces the basis toward zero at contract expiration, a process called *convergence*. Specifically, with arbitrage-free pricing, the futures and spot prices will converge so that the futures price for same-day delivery equals the spot price.

The difference between a near-term (time $t_1$) and a longer-term (time $t_2$) futures price on the same underlying asset, $F_0^1 - F_0^2$, is called the *calendar spread*. As with the basis, the calendar spread will be positive if the cash flows from the underlying asset exceed the opportunity costs of funds:

$$\text{Spread} = F_0^1 - F_0^2 = S_0 \left[ (1 + r)^{t_1} - (1 + r)^{t_2} \right] + CF_1 - CF_2. \qquad (2.10)$$

But for an underlying asset with zero expected cash flow, the definition of spread is sometimes reversed so that the spread can be quoted as a positive number:

$$\text{Spread} = F_0^2 - F_0^1 = S_0 \left[ (1 + r)^{t_2} - (1 + r)^{t_1} \right]. \qquad (2.11)$$

**Figure 2.1** illustrates how, for an underlying asset with a zero expected cash flow, the basis declines over time. The basis of the near-term contract declines to zero at time $t_1$, the near-term expiration date, whereas the calendar spread between the two contracts remains relatively constant. The basis of the longer-term contract, which is the sum of the near-term contract basis and the calendar spread, also declines over time but does not converge to zero until time $t_2$, the expiration date of the longer-term contract.

For numerical examples of basis and calendar spread, consider the June and September Mini S&P 500 futures contracts in Table 2.2. Because the S&P 500 Index provides a significant expected cash flow in the form of dividends, we measure the basis of the near-term contract as the spot minus futures price:

$$\text{Basis} = S_0 - F_0^1 = 1,330.66 - 1,328.25 = 2.41,$$

a value that will slowly converge toward zero as the June settlement date approaches. As discussed in the section on the Mini S&P 500 contracts, the relative values of the spot and futures prices are indicative of one-month interest rates available on 15 May 2012 and the expected dividend yield. The

**Figure 2.1. Futures Contract Basis and Calendar Spread**

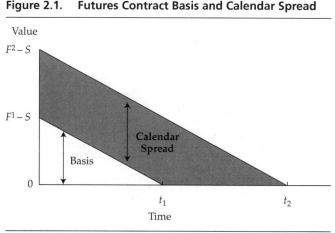

calendar spread between the September and June Mini S&P 500 contracts in Table 2.2 is

$$\text{Spread} = F_0^2 - F_0^1 = 1{,}328.25 - 1{,}321.75 = 6.50,$$

which should remain fairly constant for the life of the near-term contract. The relative prices of the September and June contracts, together with the S&P 500 dividend yield, are, in fact, indicative of the three-month forward interest rate starting on 15 June that investors can lock into on 15 May.

Whereas a contract's basis is defined as a simple difference in prices, a related concept is the *ratio* of the futures price to the spot price, $F_0 / S_0$, which remains fairly constant, even with large movements in the price of the underlying asset. Specifically, if the underlying asset has zero expected cash flow, the arbitrage-free ratio of the futures price to the spot price is

$$\frac{F_0}{S_0} = (1+r)^t, \tag{2.12}$$

which converges toward 1.0 as the contract nears expiration.

As we discuss in the next chapter, the insensitivity of this ratio to sudden changes in the spot price makes the futures contract a good hedging instrument for investors with an exposure to the underlying asset. Although options contracts can also be used to hedge risk, the reader will see in later chapters that the ratio of an option price to the price of the underlying asset can change dramatically with the price of the underlying asset. Similarly, whereas the calendar spread is typically defined as a simple difference, the *ratio* of the longer-term to near-term futures contract prices, $F_0^2 / F_0^1$, remains fairly constant over time, despite potentially large movements in the price of the underlying asset. The stability of this ratio facilitates rolling a hedge over from one futures contract to another as the near-term contract expires.

# 3. Futures Contracts: Hedging Relationships

Futures can be used to provide leveraged exposure to an asset or asset class or to control, and potentially eliminate, the risk of the underlying asset. This chapter focuses on the use of futures to offset risk by "hedging" an investment position. The first section describes a general framework to illustrate the essential characteristics of hedging. Subsequent sections discuss specific applications of the general framework.

## Net Price Created by a Hedge

Suppose an investor currently (Time 0) holds an asset priced at $S_0$. To hedge the risk of price changes for that asset, the investor sells a futures contract at a price of $F_0$. At time $t$, the security is worth $S_t$, the futures contract has a price of $F_t$, and the basis is the difference between the two prices, as shown in **Table 3.1**.

**Table 3.1  Futures Basis**

|  | Security | Futures | Basis |
|---|---|---|---|
| Now (time 0) | $S_0$ | $F_0$ | $S_0 - F_0$ |
| Later (time $t$) | $S_t$ | $F_t$ | $S_t - F_t$ |

We next discuss various ways the value of the total hedged position (security and short futures contract) at time $t$ can be described using these variables.

One way to express the final value of the hedged position, $P_t$, is the price of the underlying security at time $t$, plus the gain or loss on the short futures contract:

$$P_t = S_t + \left(F_0 - F_t\right)$$
$$= \text{Ending security price} + \text{Short futures gain}. \tag{3.1}$$

A rearrangement of the variables gives the value of the hedged position at time $t$ in two other, equivalent forms. First, Equation 3.2 shows that the value of the hedged position is the futures price at Time 0 plus the basis at time $t$:

$$P_t = F_0 + \left(S_t - F_t\right)$$
$$= \text{Initial futures price} + \text{Ending basis}. \tag{3.2}$$

Second, Equation 3.3 shows that the value of the hedged position can be thought of as the security price at Time 0 plus the change in the basis between Time 0 and time $t$:

$$P_t = S_0 + \left[ (S_t - F_t) - (S_0 - F_0) \right]$$

(3.3)

$$= \text{Initial security price} + \text{Change in basis.}$$

All three forms are equivalent ways of expressing the value an investor creates by hedging an underlying security using a futures contract.

Perhaps the most intuitive interpretation of the three expressions relative to the notion of hedging is the second, Equation 3.2, in which the value of the hedged position is equal to the current price of the futures contract plus the basis at time $t$. Specifically, an investor who sells a futures contract agrees to sell the underlying asset at the now-current futures price. On the one hand, if the time horizon for the hedge is equal to the expiration date of the futures contract, then the ending basis at that date is generally zero. In this case, the value of the hedged position is equal to the current futures price no matter what subsequently happens to the price of the underlying security. In other words, the investor has created a riskless position by holding the underlying security and selling a futures contract. On the other hand, if the time to expiration of the futures contract exceeds the hedge horizon, the net carrying cost for the holding period is different from what is implied in the current futures price. Consequently, the value differs from the price of the current futures contract by the remaining portion of the net carrying cost reflected in the basis at time $t$. Thus, a hedged position reduces the fundamental price risk in the underlying security to the price risk in the basis, as shown in Equation 3.2. Based on the intuition of this expression, using a futures contract to hedge is sometimes referred to as *speculation in the basis*.

Alternatively, the investor can think of the value of the hedged position as equal to the current price of the security plus the change in the basis between Time 0 and time $t$, as shown in Equation 3.3. The convergence of the futures contract price to the security price over time makes the hedged value differ from the current cash price of the security by the convergence in the basis.

Perhaps the most common hedging scenario is when an investor sells a futures contract to hedge the price risk of an underlying asset. Because the asset is already in the investor's portfolio, or "inventory," this hedge is sometimes referred to as an *inventory hedge*. An alternative scenario, which yields exactly the same interpretation, is referred to as an *anticipatory hedge*. In an anticipatory hedge, an investor purchases (i.e., establishes a long futures position in) a futures contract now, in anticipation of purchasing the underlying security at some future time $t$. At time $t$, the investor purchases the security and sells the futures contract to close out the long futures position. The net price, $P_t$, the investor will have paid for the security position will be equal to the security price minus the gain or loss on the long futures position.

The expression for this anticipatory hedge is similar to the inventory hedge developed previously, in which the net price equals the ending security price minus the futures gain/loss:

$$P_t = S_t - (F_t - F_0).$$ (3.4)

Rewriting the net price in the two additional forms shows that the investor with an anticipatory hedge can think of the net price paid for the security as being equal to the current futures price plus the ending basis,

$$P_t = F_0 + (S_t - F_t),$$ (3.5)

or, equivalently, as equal to the current security price plus the change in basis,

$$P_t = S_0 + [(S_t - F_t) - (S_0 - F_0)].$$ (3.6)

An investor who takes a position in the futures market now in anticipation of converting that position into the underlying security at time $t$ essentially creates the same price as one who buys the security now and hedges the price risk until time $t$. The two strategies are mirror images because both make a commitment to buy or sell the underlying security at time $t$. The price the market is offering the investor for delayed settlement of the transaction is the same for both strategies and is represented by the current futures price.

As a specific example of an anticipatory hedge, suppose an investor expects to receive funds in two months that will then be deposited to earn the Eurodollar rate. Fearing that interest rates may fall between now and then, the investor decides to hedge by purchasing Eurodollar futures now. Suppose the market currently offers a futures price of 98.5, which represents an annualized interest rate of 100 − 98.5 = 1.5%. The current spot price for Eurodollar deposits is 98.2, which represents an interest rate of 100 − 98.2 = 1.8%. In two months, suppose Eurodollar rates have fallen to 1.1% and the futures price has thus risen 0.4 points to 98.9, as shown in **Table 3.2**.

**Table 3.2    Futures Basis Example**

|                  | Security | Futures | Basis |
|------------------|----------|---------|-------|
| Now              | 98.2     | 98.5    | −0.3  |
| Two months later | 98.9     | 98.9    | 0.0   |
| Net change       | 0.7      | 0.4     | 0.3   |

The gain of 0.4 points on the futures contract serves to increase the net interest rate the investor will receive over and above the then-current rate of 1.1%. Using Equations 3.4, 3.5, and 3.6 for the net price at time $t$ gives

$P_t$ = Ending security price − Futures gain = 98.9 − 0.4 = 98.5

$P_t$ = Beginning futures price + Ending basis = 98.5 − 0.0 = 98.5

$P_t$ = Beginning security price + Change in basis = 98.2 + 0.3 = 98.5.

The net price of 98.5 allows the investor to enjoy an interest rate of 100 − 98.5 = 1.5%, even though rates had fallen to 1.1% when the investment was made. Of course, interest rates might have increased over the two-month period, in which case the anticipatory hedge would have incurred a loss that offsets the potentially higher interest rate. Note that the expiration date of the futures contract in this example is also the date at which the investor plans to invest, so the basis has completely converged to zero. If the expiration date of the futures contract were longer than two months, the basis probably would not have completely converged to zero and the hedge would still contain some basis risk.

In summary, the price the hedger receives when constructing an inventory hedge for an existing security position, or when constructing an anticipatory hedge for an intended position, is equal to the current futures price plus whatever the basis is at the termination of the hedge. By using interest rate hedging, the investor locks in the interest rate implied by the futures contract rather than the current spot interest rate. The promise of delayed settlement is offered by the market at the futures price, which will not be equal to the current spot price unless the net cost of carry happens to be zero.

## Synthetic Securities

Another way to think about the use of futures contracts is that cash-and-carry arbitrage ensures that the futures contract plus a cash reserve behaves like the underlying security:

Futures + Cash ↔ Security

Specifically, an investor may wish to create the same risk–return profile as the underlying security but use a futures contract because the transaction can often be done more quickly and at less cost than buying or selling the underlying security. Such a process can be thought of as creating a *synthetic security* in place of the actual security.

As shown in Table 2.2, the S&P 500 Index was at 1,330.66 on Tuesday, 15 May 2012. Three weeks later, on Tuesday, 5 June, the index had fallen to 1,285.54, for a loss of 1,285.54/1,330.66 − 1 = −3.39%. Dividends received on the S&P 500 stocks over this three-week period amounted to about $1.60, so the total return to an investor in the S&P 500 portfolio was (1,285.54 + 1.60)/1,330.66 − 1 = −3.27%.

The quotes in **Table 3.3** can be used to illustrate the parallel performance of the underlying security and the synthetic security created by using the futures market plus a cash reserve. The investor puts the same dollar amount as the security purchase, $1,330.66, into a cash reserve paying interest of 1 bp (basis point) per week and purchases a futures contract. Three weeks later, the synthetic security will have a value of 1,331.06 + (1,285.00 − 1,328.25) = 1,287.81 and a return of 1,287.81/1,330.66 − 1 = −3.22%. The 3.22% return is composed of a 0.03% return on the cash reserve for three weeks and a −3.25% price change from the equity futures contract relative to the underlying index. The arbitrage between the futures contract and the underlying index keeps the futures price in a relationship so that the returns to the underlying and synthetic security will be similar. Small differences can sometimes occur, as in this case, because of tracking error between the index and the futures contract.

**Table 3.3     Synthetic Equity Using Futures Contracts**

|  | Price Now (15 May) | Price Three Weeks Later (5 June) | Percentage Change |
|---|---|---|---|
| Cash reserve | $1,330.66 | $1,331.06 | 0.03 |
| Equity futures | 1,328.25 | 1,285.00 | −3.25 |
| Futures + Cash | 1,330.66 | 1,287.81 | −3.22 |

The basic arbitrage relationship can also be written to express the creation of "synthetic cash" as well as a synthetic security. In fact, creating a synthetic cash position is nothing more than creating an inventory hedge:

$$\boxed{\text{Security}} - \boxed{\text{Futures}} \leftrightarrow \boxed{\text{Cash}}$$

The cash-and-carry arbitrage relationship keeps the futures contract priced so that an offsetting position relative to the underlying security results in a return consistent with a riskless rate. In essence, creating a hedged position eliminates the primary risk in the underlying security by shifting it to others willing to bear the risk. Of course, the risk could be eliminated directly by simply selling the underlying security position, but this step might interfere with the nature of the investor's business, disrupt a continuing investment program, or incur unwanted transaction costs or taxes. Thus, the futures market can provide an alternate way to temporarily offset or eliminate much of the risk in the underlying security position.

**Table 3.4** shows the effect of hedging the risk of an equity portfolio that tracks the S&P 500. As mentioned previously, over the three weeks following 15 May 2012, the S&P 500 fell by 3.39% and the June (near-term) futures contract price fell by 3.25%. If the portfolio had been hedged by shorting the futures contract, the net value would be $1,285.54 - (1,285.00 - 1,328.25) = 1,285.54 + 43.25 = 1,328.79$, or a return of $1,28.79/1,330.66 - 1 = -0.14\%$ before dividends. If only half of the portfolio had been hedged, the net value would be $1,285.54 + 43.25/2 = 1,307.17$, for a return of $1,307.17/1,330.66 - 1 = -1.77\%$, compared with $-3.39\%$ for the S&P 500. Using the futures market allows an investor to temporarily eliminate some or all of the price risk in the equity portfolio, equivalent to altering the beta. A partial hedge would reduce the beta below 1.00, and a complete hedge would reduce the beta to zero.

**Table 3.4   Synthetic Cash Using Futures Contracts**

|  | Price Now (15 May) | Price Three Weeks Later (5 June) | Percentage Change |
|---|---|---|---|
| Equity security | $1,330.66 | $1,285.54 | -3.39 |
| Equity futures | 1,328.25 | 1,285.00 | -3.25 |
| Security – Futures | 1,330.66 | 1,328.79 | -0.14 |

A different way of looking at the creation of synthetic cash is to calculate the repo rate implied in the pricing of the futures contract. From Chapter 2, we know that the arbitrage-free price of an equity futures contract is given by Equation 2.3—namely,

$$F_0 = S_0 (1+r)^t - D_t, \tag{3.7}$$

where $t$ is the time to maturity of the futures contract measured in years (e.g., $t = 1/12$ for one month) and $D_t$ denotes the dividends paid on the underlying index until the expiration date. Solving for the implied repo rate in this formula gives

$$r = \left( \frac{F_0 + D_t}{S_0} \right)^{1/t} - 1. \tag{3.8}$$

Thus, the implied repo rate of the S&P 500 futures contract for the June expiration is

$$r = \left( \frac{1328.25 + 1.60}{1330.66} \right)^{12} - 1 = -0.73\%.$$

Although interest rates were at historically low values in 2012, they were not negative, indicating that the futures contract is a bit underpriced. In theory, an investor could have captured an arbitrage profit by shorting the stocks in the index and buying the underpriced futures contract, although the costs of shorting together with transaction costs on both the spot index and futures contract might have been larger than the potential arbitrage profit. If an arbitrage is too costly to implement, the futures price may deviate slightly from its fair value.

The impact of partial or complete hedging can also be seen by examining the effect on a portfolio's return profile and return probability distribution. **Figure 3.1** illustrates the return on the hedged portfolio relative to the return on the underlying security. A partial hedge position reduces the slope of the return line, so the hedged portfolio does not perform as well as the underlying security when returns are high but also does not perform as poorly when returns are low. The greater the portion of the portfolio that is hedged, the lower the slope of the line. A full hedge produces a flat line, indicating that the hedged portfolio will generate a fixed return no matter what the underlying asset does. This fixed return should be equal to the riskless rate if the futures contract is fairly priced.

**Figure 3.2** shows how the addition of a futures hedge changes the probability distribution of returns. If the return distribution for the underlying security is symmetrical, with a wide dispersion, hedging the portfolio with futures gradually draws both tails of the distribution in toward the middle and the mean return moves toward the riskless rate. A full futures hedge draws both

**Figure 3.1. Return Profiles for Hedged Portfolios**

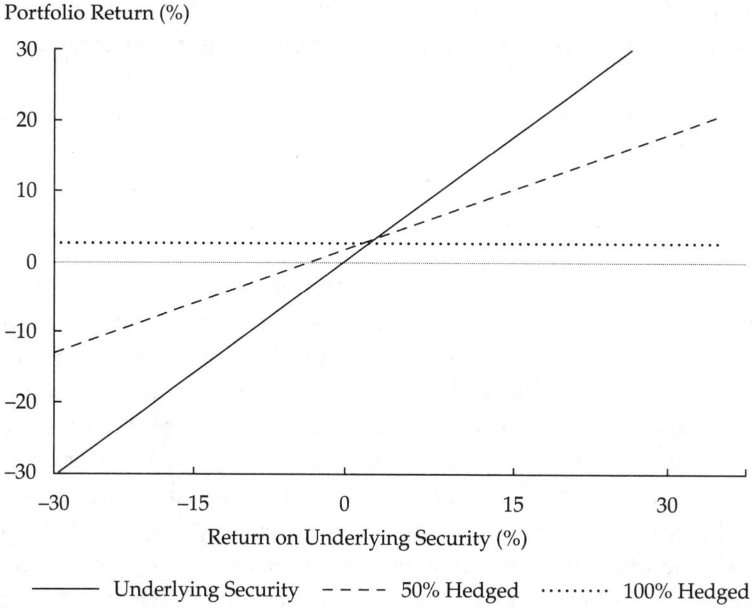

Portfolio Return (%)

Return on Underlying Security (%)

——— Underlying Security    – – – 50% Hedged    ········· 100% Hedged

**Figure 3.2. Return Distribution for Hedged Portfolios**

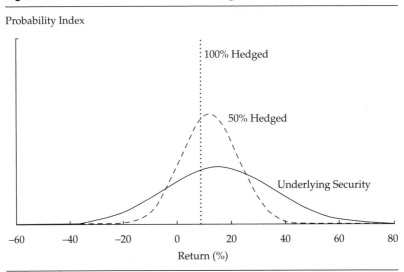

tails in and puts all of the probability mass at the riskless rate. As the reader will see in Chapter 4, options generally affect one tail more dramatically than the other, so the distribution of a portfolio hedged with options becomes quite skewed, in contrast to the more symmetrical impact of hedging with futures.

## The Choice of Contract Maturity

An additional issue to consider is what maturity to use for the futures contract in constructing the hedge position. If the hedging horizon extends beyond the expiration of the nearby futures contract, the hedger using the nearby contract must switch over to the deferred futures contract at some point to maintain the hedge. Thus, the investor has a choice of initiating the hedge by using the nearby contract and then rolling forward at some point into the longer-term contract, which is called a *stack hedge*, or using the longer-term contract right from the start, which is called a *strip hedge*.

Rolling the hedge forward requires that an investor sell a nearby contract with one maturity and buy a deferred contract at some date prior to the expiration of the nearby contract. **Figure 3.3** illustrates the time frame for the construction of the stack hedge. In Figure 3.3, $t$ is the rollover date, $t_1$ is the nearby contract expiration date, $T$ is the hedge horizon, and $t_2$ is the longer-term contract expiration date. Note that an investor who initiates a stack hedge with the nearby contract is exposed to the price risk of rolling the nearby contract over into the deferred contract on rollover date $t$. Although the deferred contract may have the disadvantage of less liquidity than the nearby contract, a strip hedge that uses only the deferred contract is

**Figure 3.3. Hedging Time Frame**

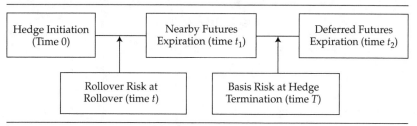

not exposed to this rollover risk. Both the stack and strip hedge are exposed, however, to the eventual basis risk associated with termination of the hedge prior to the longer-term futures contract expiration date, $t_2$.

**Figure 3.4** illustrates the difference between the contract positions needed for the stack and for the strip. A hedge created using the deferred contract initially places all the positions into that contract. That position is maintained throughout the course of the hedge, so no further changes need to be made. A stack hedge created using the nearby contract first establishes positions in the nearby contract and then rolls them forward into the deferred contract before the nearby contract expires. At Time 0, the calendar spread that will exist between the two contracts on the date of the forward roll, $t$, is uncertain, so the net price that the investor receives with a stack hedge will incorporate that risk, in addition to the basis risk, at time $T$ when the hedge is terminated.

To further examine the relative risks of each hedge structure, consider the net price received at the termination of the hedge under the strip strategy, which uses only the deferred contract. The net price for the hedger is the ending spot price plus the gain in the deferred contract during the life of the hedge or, equivalently, the current price of the longer-term contract plus its ending spot–futures basis:

$$P_T(\text{Strip}) = S_T + \left(F_0^2 - F_T^2\right) = F_0^2 + \left(S_T - F_T^2\right). \tag{3.9}$$

The second formulation in Equation 3.9 shows that the risk of the strip hedge is caused by the uncertainty of the longer-term contract's basis at time $T$, the termination of the hedge. If the hedge termination is close enough to the longer-term contract expiration date, this basis risk will be small and will theoretically, under arbitrage-free pricing, converge to zero on the contract expiration date.

Now, consider the stack hedge that first uses the nearby contract and is then rolled into the deferred contract at time $t$. In the stack hedge, the net price is a function of the gain or loss on both futures contracts. An equivalent formulation for the net price of the stack hedge is the current price of the

**Figure 3.4.    Stack vs. Strip Contract Positions**

*A. Strip Hedge*

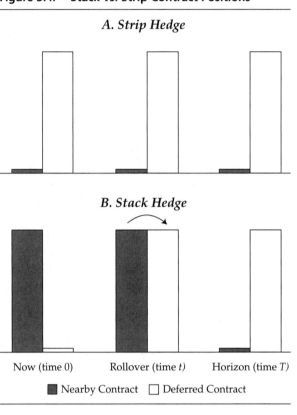

*B. Stack Hedge*

Now (time 0)         Rollover (time *t*)         Horizon (time *T*)

■ Nearby Contract   □ Deferred Contract

nearby contract plus the calendar spread on the date of the roll plus the ending basis of the longer-term contract:

$$P_T(\text{Stack}) = S_T + \left(F_0^1 - F_t^1\right) + \left(F_t^2 - F_T^2\right) = F_0^1 - \left(F_t^1 - F_t^2\right) + \left(S_T - F_T^2\right). \tag{3.10}$$

The second formulation in Equation 3.10 shows that there are two sources of uncertainty for the net price of the stack hedge: the risk of the contract roll (or calendar spread) at time *t* and the basis risk of the longer-term contract at time *T*, the termination of the hedge. Combining Equations 3.9 and 3.10 shows that the difference between the net price of the stack hedge and the net price of the strip hedge depends on the calendar spread between the two contracts at the time of the forward roll relative to the spread now:

$$P_T(\text{Strip}) - P_T(\text{Stack}) = \left(F_0^1 - F_0^2\right) - \left(F_t^1 - F_t^2\right). \tag{3.11}$$

Thus, the stack will result in a lower net price to the hedger if the calendar spread is wider on the date of the roll than at the initiation of the hedge. The strip gives the investor the chance to roll the hedge into the longer-maturity contract at a wider spread, but it also entails the risk that the spread may be narrower. Because calendar spreads are, in part, a function of interest rates, using the stack exposes the hedge to interest rate risk at time $t$.

As a numerical illustration of the net prices for a stack versus a strip hedge, consider the S&P 500 spot and mini futures prices listed in **Table 3.5**.

**Table 3.5    Spot and S&P 500 Futures Prices on Three Dates**

|  | Time 0 (15 May) | Time $t$ (5 June) | Time $T$ (26 June) |
|---|---|---|---|
| S&P 500 spot price, $S$ | $1,330.66 | $1,285.54 | $1,319.99 |
| June contract, $F^1$ | 1,328.25 | 1,285.00 | — |
| September contract, $F^2$ | 1,321.75 | 1,278.50 | 1,315.50 |

An investor wants to hedge the risk of an S&P 500 portfolio for the six weeks from 15 May (Time 0) to 26 June (time $T$). The investor can use the longer-term September contract for this hedge or use the nearby June contract with a rollover to the longer-term contract sometime prior to the 15 June expiration date. The net price of the strip hedge using Equation 3.9 is

$$P_T(\text{Strip}) = S_T + \left(F_0^2 - F_T^2\right) = 1,319.99 + 6.25 = 1,326.24.$$

Alternatively, suppose the investor chooses the stack hedge and rolls the hedge into the September contract on 5 June (time $t$). The net price using the stack hedge is

$$P_T(\text{Stack}) = S_T + \left(F_0^1 - F_t^1\right) + \left(F_t^2 - F_T^2\right) = 1,319.99 + 43.25 - 37.00 = 1,326.24.$$

Although no difference resulted between the two hedging strategies in this numerical example, the potential difference can be described as the change in the calendar spread between the initiation of the hedge at Time 0 and the forward roll at time $t$:

$$\left(F_0^1 - F_0^2\right) - \left(F_t^1 - F_t^2\right) = 6.50 - 6.50 = 0.00.$$

In other words, the net prices of the stack and strip hedges are equal in this example because the calendar spread did not change between the date the hedge was initiated and the date of the rollover. But changes in calendar spread are possible if unanticipated changes in interest rates or dividend yields occur or if one or the other futures contract deviates substantially from arbitrage-free pricing.

## A Generalized Hedging Framework

The previous section presented a simple framework to illustrate the basics of using a generic futures contract to hedge a position in an underlying security. In this simple framework, we assumed that a single contract was the appropriate position to take for the purpose of hedging. But a single exchange-traded contract will generally not match the exact dollar amount of underlying exposure the investor desires. In addition, the available futures contracts (e.g., S&P 500 futures) may not be perfectly correlated with the investor's exposure (e.g., a large-capitalization domestic equity portfolio), necessitating what is commonly called a *cross-hedge*. With a cross-hedge, a dollar position in the futures contract that is equal to the dollar size of the investor's asset exposure may not be the optimal hedge. This section discusses hedging in a framework that accommodates these more involved situations and then applies that general framework to a variety of specific futures contracts and underlying securities.

To set up the general framework, we start with an investor who wants to hedge the value of some asset or security over the short term with a futures position. Specifically, the hedge is composed of a security priced at $S$ plus $h$ futures contracts valued at $F$. In this context, $h$ is called the *hedge ratio* and will generally be a negative number to represent a *short* futures position. The change in the hedged value over time as a function of changes in the security price and the futures price is

$$\Delta V = \Delta S + h \Delta F. \tag{3.12}$$

Solving for the hedge ratio gives

$$h = \frac{\Delta V - \Delta S}{\Delta F}. \tag{3.13}$$

The special case of the hedge ratio that completely eliminates the short-term price risk, so that $\Delta V = 0$, is thus

$$h = \frac{-\Delta S}{\Delta F}. \tag{3.14}$$

The short-term hedge in Equation 3.14 might need to be modified to allow for convergence in the spot–futures basis over a longer time horizon, and it assumes that the investor wants the most complete hedge possible. Nevertheless, the result is intuitively helpful. For example, suppose $S$ is some well-diversified equity portfolio and $F$ is the S&P 500 futures contract. If the equity portfolio was, in fact, the S&P 500 Index portfolio, then the arbitrage-free pricing conditions outlined in Chapter 2 would dictate that the change in the futures price be approximately equal to the change in the spot price, $\Delta F = \Delta S$, and the short-term hedge ratio would be –1.00. But in general, even a well-diversified but actively managed large-cap U.S. equity portfolio will not track the S&P 500 exactly. For example, suppose the beta of the managed portfolio with respect to the S&P 500 is 0.95 with an additional active risk of 3.0% per year. In that scenario,

$$\Delta S = 0.95(\Delta F)$$

and the hedge ratio is

$$h = \frac{-\Delta S}{\Delta F} = -0.95.$$

In this example, an investor would sell futures contracts worth 95% of the value of the equity portfolio. The hedge would eliminate the short-term market risk of the portfolio, although not the remaining active risk of 3.0%. Alternatively, the investor might want to hedge only a portion of the market risk. For example, the investor might decide to implement a hedge targeted at 60% rather than 100% of the market risk, $\Delta V = 0.6(\Delta S)$. In this scenario, the hedge ratio would be

$$h = \frac{\Delta V - \Delta S}{\Delta F} = (0.60 - 1.00)0.95 = -0.38.$$

That is, the investor would sell futures contracts worth only 38% of the value of the equity portfolio.

The first key point is that most hedges are, in fact, cross-hedges because the futures contract does not perfectly replicate the price movement of the underlying security. A hedge can still be created, but the link between price movements in the futures contract and the underlying security position will not be exact, leaving residual risk, or noise, in the relationship. The second key point is that hedges that completely eliminate market risk are at one end of the hedging spectrum, with completely unhedged positions at the other end and a variety of partial hedges in between.

## The Minimum-Variance Hedge Ratio

The hedge ratio that minimizes the variance of the net exposure is sometimes referred to as the *minimum-variance hedge ratio*. The minimum-variance hedge ratio can be based on the conceptual arbitrage relationship or determined empirically using regression analysis on historical data. Regression analysis usually provides a reasonable value for the minimum-variance hedge ratio. But depending on the length of the measurement period, the number of periods used, and the assumed stability of the pricing process over the historical period, that estimate can differ from the ratio based on the conceptual arbitrage relationship discussed here.

The hedge ratio needed to minimize the residual risk can be derived from the generalized hedging structure described by Equation 3.12. Taking the variance of returns and allowing for less-than-perfect correlation between the returns on the security price, $S$, and the futures contract price, $F$, gives

$$\sigma_V^2 = \sigma_S^2 + h^2 \sigma_F^2 + 2h\sigma_S \sigma_F \rho_{SF}, \tag{3.15}$$

where $\sigma_S$ and $\sigma_F$ are the volatilities of, respectively, the security and futures contract returns and $\rho_{SF}$ is the correlation coefficient between the security and futures contract returns.

Taking the first derivative of Equation 3.15 with respect to the hedge ratio, $h$, and setting the result equal to zero gives the minimum-variance hedge as

$$h = -\rho_{SF} \frac{\sigma_S}{\sigma_F}. \tag{3.16}$$

Substituting Equation 3.16 back into Equation 3.15 gives the variance of the hedged position as

$$\sigma_V^2 = \sigma_S^2 (1 - \rho_{SF}^2). \tag{3.17}$$

Thus, if the returns on the security and the futures contract used in the hedge are perfectly correlated, so that the value of $\rho_{SF}$ is zero, then the variance of the net exposure in Equation 3.17 is zero, indicating that the risk of the underlying security can be completely hedged.

In general, correlation between the security and the futures returns will be less than perfect, leaving some amount of residual risk. The minimum-variance hedge converts the price risk of the security into the smaller tracking error between the security and the futures contract. For example, consider the simple case in which the risks of the security and futures contracts are equal, $\sigma_S = \sigma_F$, so that the optimal hedge in Equation 3.16 is the negative value of the correlation coefficient, $h = -\rho_{SF}$. If the correlation is less than perfect— say, $\rho_{SF} = 0.90$—the optimal hedge ratio is −0.90 and the ratio of hedged variance to security variance in Equation 3.17 is $1 - 0.90^2 = 0.19$, meaning that the minimum-variance hedge has only 19% of the variance of the unhedged position. For a lower correlation—say, $\rho_{SF} = 0.80$—the remaining variance is $1 - 0.80^2 = 36\%$ of the variance of the unhedged position, even after the optimal hedge has been applied.

The minimum-variance hedge ratio is sometimes estimated statistically by regressing the underlying security returns on the futures contract returns. Specifically, the negative of the slope coefficient from the regression produces an estimate of the minimum-variance hedge ratio. Although this time-series regression technique is often used to estimate the appropriate hedge ratio, care must be taken in interpreting the results. Because the regression usually incorporates returns for several successive days or weeks, the regression generally does not account for the slow but inevitable convergence of the futures contract and the underlying spot price. The typical regression will calculate a hedge ratio that averages the futures return variance over the past life of the contract, not the variance at the initiation of the hedge. Examination of the arbitrage-free futures price as a function of the underlying spot price in Chapter 2 indicates, however, that changes in price of the futures when the expiration date on the futures is still far away will be different from changes when the contract is about to expire. For many cross-hedging applications, this distortion will be small and unimportant. But for some applications, such as pure arbitrage against the spot price, precision will be more critical and the time-series regression analysis will not be adequate.

## Theoretical Hedge Ratios

As discussed in Chapter 2, the arbitrage relationship between a futures contract and the index on which the futures contract is based keeps the prices tightly linked together. Here, we show how this arbitrage relationship can be combined with a measure of an asset's responsiveness to the underlying index to determine the optimal hedge ratio. This hedge ratio, together with the notional value of the futures contract, can then be used to calculate the number of futures contracts needed for the optimal hedge. We consider theoretical hedge ratios for three kinds of investor exposures: equity portfolio hedges, bond hedges, and foreign currency hedges.

**Equity Portfolio Hedges.** Suppose the price of an investor's equity portfolio changes by a factor of $\beta$ relative to the index used by the futures contract,

$$\Delta S = \beta \Delta I, \tag{3.18}$$

where $I$ represents the index. As shown in Chapter 2, in an arbitrage-free market, the price change in the futures contract, $\Delta F$, with respect to the price change in the market index, $\Delta I$, is given by

$$\Delta F = \Delta I \left(1+r-d\right)^{t}, \tag{3.19}$$

where $t$ is the time to contract expiration (measured in years) and $r$ and $d$ are, respectively, the annualized short-term interest rate and index dividend yield. Inserting the two relationships in Equations 3.18 and 3.19 into the general optimal hedge ratio in Equation 3.14 gives

$$h = \frac{-\beta}{\left(1+r-d\right)^{t}}. \tag{3.20}$$

Together with the notional value of a single futures contract and the dollar value of the investor's portfolio, the optimal hedge ratio in Equation 3.20 can be used to determine the number of futures contracts to buy or sell.

As an example, consider the calculation of the minimum-variance hedge ratio and the number of futures contracts required for a short-term (e.g., three-day) hedge of a $22 million equity portfolio with a beta of exactly 1.0 relative to the S&P 500. If the short-term interest rate is 0.50%, the dividend yield is 2.50%, and the futures contract has three months to expiration ($t = 0.25$), the optimal hedge ratio in Equation 3.20 is

$$h = -\frac{1.0}{(1 + 0.0050 - 0.0250)^{0.25}} = -1.005.$$

Because the futures contract's expiration date of three months is well beyond the short-term investment horizon of three days, the hedge ratio is not an equal dollar match even when the beta of the equity portfolio is exactly 1.00. Note that the exact value of this optimal hedge ratio can change after a day or two, but the convergence in basis from one day to the next is quite small. As shown in Table 1.1, the contract size for the Mini S&P 500 futures is 50 times the value of the S&P 500. Suppose the index is currently at 1,330, so the notional value is $50 \times 1,330 = \$66,500$ per contract. Then, the number of Mini S&P 500 contracts required for an optimal short-term hedge of the $22 million equity portfolio is

$$n = h\left(\frac{\text{Value hedged}}{\text{Contract size}}\right) = -1.005\left(\frac{22,000,000}{66,500}\right) = -332.5,$$

where the minus sign indicates a short futures position.

In contrast, if the investor wanted to hedge the risk of the equity portfolio for three months, the hedge ratio would be 1.000 and the number of contracts needed would be slightly lower:

$$n = h\left(\frac{\text{Value hedged}}{\text{Contract size}}\right) = -1.000\left(\frac{22,000,000}{66,500}\right) = -330.8.$$

Note that this difference in optimal hedge ratios depending on the investment horizon (i.e., three days or three months) may not be considered material relative to the basis risk in the hedge and, consequently, is often disregarded by investors.

**Bond Hedges.** To illustrate the hedging of a bond, we will use the fixed-income concept of duration, similar to using an equity portfolio's beta in an equity hedge. The modified duration of a bond, $D_B^*$, is defined as the negative percentage change in bond price, $-\Delta B/B$, associated with a change in the bond's yield, $\Delta y_B$,

$$-\frac{\Delta B}{B} = D_B^* \Delta y_B. \tag{3.21}$$

The minus sign is used in Equation 3.21 because a bond's price and yield move in opposite directions. Similarly, the modified duration of a bond futures contract, $D_F^*$, is

$$-\left(\frac{\Delta F}{F}\right) = D_F^* \, \Delta y_F, \tag{3.22}$$

where $F$ represents the futures price and $y_F$ is the yield to maturity of the futures contract's cheapest-to-deliver (CTD) bond.

Using the concept of duration as defined in Equations 3.21 and 3.22 in the general optimal hedge ratio in Equation 3.14 gives

$$h = -\frac{D_B^*}{D_F^*}\left(\frac{B}{F}\right)\left(\frac{\Delta y_B}{\Delta y_F}\right). \tag{3.23}$$

To illustrate the calculation of this hedge ratio, we will use a \$28 million bond position hedged with T-note futures. Suppose the futures price is 133 12/32 (133.375% of par), the bond price is 138 16/32 (138.500% of par), and the modified durations of the security and the futures contract are, respectively, 10.3 years and 9.4 years. In this example, we assume that the ratio of the change in yield to maturity of the bond being hedged to the change of the future's contract CTD bond is $\Delta y_B / \Delta y_F = 0.98$.

With these numbers, the optimal hedge ratio in Equation 3.23 is

$$h = -\frac{10.3}{9.4}\left(\frac{138.500}{133.375}\right)(0.98) = -1.115.$$

As shown in Table 1.1, the notional value of each Treasury note futures contract is \$100,000 times the price of the CTD bond. If the price of the CTD bond is 132.750% of par, the notional value of each contract is \$132,750. So, the optimal hedge on the \$28 million bond exposure would require

$$n = h\left(\frac{\text{Value hedged}}{\text{Contract size}}\right) = -1.115\left(\frac{28,000,000}{132,750}\right) = -235.2$$

contracts, where, again, the negative value indicates a short futures position.

A concept closely related to duration is DV01, defined as the dollar value of the change in the fair value of a security or portfolio arising from a 1 bp change in interest rates. As discussed in the appendix, DV01 is often used instead of more general duration numbers to calculate the number of futures contracts needed for a hedge.

**Foreign Exchange Hedges.** As discussed in Chapter 2, the arbitrage-free price of currency futures depends on the relative values of the domestic and foreign interest rates. Using Equation 2.7, the *change* in the currency futures price given a *change* in the spot exchange rate (quoted as domestic currency per foreign currency unit—e.g., USD/EUR), is

$$\Delta F = \Delta S \left( \frac{1+r_d}{1+r_f} \right)^t,$$  (3.24)

where

    $t$ = time to contract expiration (measured in years)
    $r_d$ = domestic short-term interest rate
    $r_f$ = foreign short-term interest rate
The optimal hedge ratio given in Equation 3.14 applied to the specific case currency hedges is, therefore,

$$h = -\left( \frac{1+r_f}{1+r_d} \right)^t.$$  (3.25)

Thus, the optimal hedge ratio will be slightly different from 1.0 for any material difference between the two interest rates and a long enough expiration date for the futures contract.

As an example of how to use currency futures in a short-term hedge, consider a U.S. investor with a €5 million exposure. Suppose the domestic short-term interest rate is 3.75%, the euro interest rate is 1.25%, and the futures contract has six months to expiration. Then, the optimal hedge ratio is

$$h = -\left( \frac{1+0.0125}{1+0.0375} \right)^{0.50} = -0.988.$$

As shown in Table 1.1, the contract size for the USD/EUR futures is €125,000, so the hedge on a €5,000,000 exposure requires

$$n = h\left( \frac{\text{Value hedged}}{\text{Contract size}} \right) = -0.988 \left( \frac{5,000,000}{125,000} \right) = -39.5$$

contracts, where, again, the minus sign indicates a short futures position.

## Controlling Asset Exposure: Asset Allocation

In the previous section, we used the optimal (i.e., risk-minimizing) hedge ratio in Equation 3.14 to deal with exposures to individual assets or asset classes. Recall that the general hedging framework in Equation 3.12 defines the change in the value of a hedged portfolio as the change in the spot price, $\Delta S$, plus the hedge ratio, $h$, times the change in the future price, $\Delta F$. We close this chapter by illustrating how this general hedging relationship can be used to effectively alter the mix of stocks, bonds, and cash in a multi-asset-class portfolio. The framework can be expanded to include the foreign exchange risk embedded in an international portfolio, although for simplicity, we consider a purely domestic portfolio.

Suppose the investor has a portfolio of stocks, bonds, and cash, with weights of, respectively, $w_S$, $w_B$, and $1 - w_S - w_B$. The stock component of the portfolio has a beta of $\beta_S$ with respect to the equity index that underlies the available futures contract. The bond component has a modified duration of $D_B^*$, and the modified duration of the available fixed-income futures contract is $D_F^*$. Now, suppose the investor would like to alter the asset allocation of the portfolio to target weights of $w_S^T$ and $w_B^T$ for the stock and bond components, with the target weights set so that the modified duration of the resulting fixed-income component is $D_T^*$. Note that we assume a target beta of 1.0 for the equity component because if the investor wanted any other equity sensitivity, that result could be achieved simply by choosing a different target equity weight.

The general hedging framework in Equation 3.12 with equity-specific substitutions from Equations 3.18 and 3.19 produces the relationship

$$w_S^T \Delta I = w_S \beta_S \Delta I + h_S (1 + r - d)^t \Delta I, \tag{3.26}$$

and solving Equation 3.26 for the equity hedge ratio gives

$$h_S = \frac{w_S^T - w_S \beta_S}{(1 + r - d)^t}. \tag{3.27}$$

Similarly, the general hedging framework in Equation 3.12 with bond-specific substitutions from Equations 3.21 and 3.22 produces the relationship

$$w_B^T D_T^* B \Delta y_B = w_B D_B^* B \Delta y_B + h_B D_F^* F \Delta y_F, \tag{3.28}$$

and solving Equation 3.28 for the fixed-income hedge ratio gives

$$h_B = \left( \frac{w_B^T D_T^* - w_B D_B^*}{D_F^*} \right) \left( \frac{B}{F} \right) \left( \frac{\Delta y_B}{\Delta y_F} \right). \tag{3.29}$$

Starting with the composition and risk exposure in the physical assets, the two hedge ratios in Equations 3.27 and 3.29 allow the investor to alter the stock and bond composition and risk exposures without modifying the underlying physical asset positions. For example, the investor may be a large institution with active managers in each asset class whose security selection strategies would be disrupted by a change in the overall allocation of physical assets.

For a numerical example, suppose the investor has a $100 million portfolio composed of 60% ($60 million) stocks, 30% ($30 million) bonds, and 10% ($10 million) cash. Furthermore, the market index beta of the equity component of the portfolio is 1.1 and the duration of the fixed-income component is 8.5 years, compared with 10.3 years for the available bond futures contract.

Suppose the investor would like to target a portfolio of 50% equity and 50% fixed-income with no cash. Assume the investor's duration target remains at 8.5 years, the duration that already exists in the fixed-income component of the portfolio. If the short-term interest rate is 0.50%, the dividend yield on the index that underlies the equity futures contract is 2.50%, and the nearest available contract has three months to expiration ($t = 0.25$), the equity hedge ratio in Equation 3.27 is

$$h_S = \frac{0.50 - 0.60\,(1.1)}{(1 + 0.005 - 0.025)^{0.25}} = -0.161,$$

meaning that a short position in equity futures is required.

The actual number of equity futures contracts needed is equal to the hedge ratio times the size of the portfolio position, divided by the notional value of each futures contract. If the index is currently at 1,330, then one futures contract's notional value is $50 \times 1,330 = \$66,500$. The number of contracts required to change the exposure of the $60 million physical equity component of the total portfolio is, therefore,

$$n = -0.161\left(\frac{60,000,000}{66,500}\right) = -145.3,$$

or a short position of 145.3 contracts.

The hedge ratio required to adjust the fixed-income component of the portfolio depends on the relative prices of the average bond in the portfolio and the price of the fixed-income futures contract. Suppose the average bond price is 138 16/32 (138.500% of par), the futures price is 133 12/32 (133.375% of par), and the expected change in yield to maturity of the average bond in the portfolio is equal to the expected change in yield to maturity of the CTD bond, so $\Delta y_B / \Delta y_F = 1.0$. Then, the fixed-income hedge ratio in Equation 3.29 is

$$h_B = \left[\frac{(0.50)(8.5) - (0.30)(8.5)}{10.3}\right]\left(\frac{138.500}{133.375}\right)(1.0) = 0.171,$$

so a long position in the fixed-income futures is required.

The actual number of fixed-income futures contracts needed is equal to the hedge ratio times the size of the portfolio position, divided by the notional value of the futures contract. If the price of the CTD bond is 132.750% of par, the notional value of each contract is $132,750. Then, the number of contracts required to change the exposure of the $30 million physical fixed-income component of the portfolio is

$$n = 0.171\left(\frac{30,000,000}{132,750}\right) = 38.6.$$

Finally, note that the targeted zero cash position in the portfolio is achieved by overlaying the existing 10% cash position as part of the bond futures contracts that move the portfolio from 30% to 50% fixed-income exposure.

The principles involved in this asset allocation decision are conceptually the same as the hedging principles for individual assets developed earlier in this chapter. The ultimate goal is to determine the appropriate number of futures contracts required to produce a desired level of exposure to each underlying risk. Once the futures contracts are in place, the portfolio behaves as if the physical asset weights had been adjusted to reflect the desired asset allocation. Complete hedging eliminates all of the systematic risk, although nonhedgeable idiosyncratic risk and basis risk remain. Complete hedging is only one end of the hedging spectrum—no hedge at all being the other end, with a variety of partial hedges in between. Synthetic asset creation effectively substitutes one kind of asset-class risk for another, and as we have illustrated, futures contracts can also be used to implement tactical asset allocation. Once the investor understands how the futures contract moves relative to the underlying asset, futures contracts can be used in a variety of ways to meet investor objectives and preferences.

# 4. Option Characteristics and Strategies: Risk and Return

The two basic types of options are *call* options and *put* options. A call option gives the owner the right to buy a security at a specified price within a specified period of time. For example, a call option on the S&P 500 Index gives an investor the right to buy units of the S&P 500 at a set price within a specified amount of time. In contrast, the put option gives the owner the right to sell a security at a specified price within a particular period of time. The right, rather than obligation, to buy or sell the underlying security is what differentiates options from futures contracts. In other words, the option holder has the right to buy or not to buy, to sell or not to sell, depending on which course of action the holder deems most advantageous.

In addition to buying an option, investors may sell a call or put option they have not previously purchased, which is called *writing an option*. Thus, there are four basic option positions, as shown in **Figure 4.1**. Understanding how put and call option prices behave and how these basic option positions affect an overall portfolio is critical to understanding more complex option strategies.

**Figure 4.1.  Option Positions**

|  | Call Option | Put Option |
|---|---|---|
| Buy | Purchased the right to buy the underlying security | Purchased the right to sell the underlying security |
| Sell or Write | Sold the right to buy the underlying security (might be forced to sell) | Sold the right to sell the underlying security (might be forced to buy) |

## Option Characteristics

Options have several important characteristics, including the *strike* or *exercise price* specified in the option contract. The exercise price is the value at which the investor can purchase (with a call option) or sell (with a put option) the underlying security. The exercise price of a simple option is fixed until expiration, whereas the market price of the underlying asset naturally fluctuates.

*Moneyness* refers to the relationship between the current price of the underlying security and the option's exercise price. Specifically, for call options, the terms *in the money, at the money,* and *out of the money* identify whether the underlying security price is currently below, at, or above the option's strike or exercise price respectively. For example, a call option that has a strike price of $100 when the security price is $120 is in the money because the holder of the option can buy the security for less than its current value. For a put option, the terms in the money, at the money, and out of the money are reversed; they identify whether the underlying security price is currently below, at, or above the option's exercise price respectively. For example, a put option with a strike price of $100 while the security is priced at $90 is in the money because the investor can sell the security for more than its market price. In either case, an in-the-money option is one that currently has a positive exercise value.

A second important characteristic is the *maturity* of the option contract, which defines the time period within which the investor can buy or sell the underlying security at the exercise price. After that date, the option expires and can no longer be exercised. Option contracts come in two general types, or *styles*—those that can be exercised any time up to and including the exercise date and those that can be exercised only on the specific maturity date. An option that can be exercised early is called an *American option,* whereas an option that can be exercised only on the maturity date is called a *European option.* Although this terminology originated within a geographical context, the style terms are now used independently of where the option market is located. For example, most of the options traded on organized exchanges in the United States are American-style options, although a few European-style options are traded in the United States.

Another contract specification has to do with adjustments for any dividends or interest paid on the underlying security. An option with a strike or exercise price that is adjusted for cash distributions is called an option with *payout protection.* Most exchange-traded options on individual stocks are not protected from dividend payout but are automatically adjusted for 2-for-1, 3-for-1, and other kinds of stock splits.

The price that an exchange-traded option currently trades at, sometimes called the option's *premium,* depends on a number of factors, including the difference between the contract's strike price and the price of the underlying security. In fact, analysts have come to think of the option's market price as being composed of two parts—the *intrinsic value* and the *time value*—as illustrated in **Figure 4.2**.

The intrinsic, or exercise, value of a call option is the amount of money that would be received if an investor were to exercise the option

**Figure 4.2.  Option Price Components**

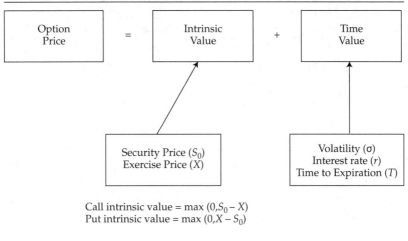

Call intrinsic value = max $(0, S_0 - X)$
Put intrinsic value = max $(0, X - S_0)$

to purchase the underlying security at the exercise price and then immediately sell the security at the current market price. In other words, the intrinsic value depends on the relationship between the current security price, $S_0$, and the exercise price of the option, $X$. If $S_0 - X$ is positive, then the call option is said to be in the money and has a positive intrinsic value. If $S_0 - X$ is negative, the call option is said to be out of the money and has zero intrinsic value. Thus, the intrinsic value of a call option is either the difference between the security price and the exercise price or zero, whichever is larger. The intrinsic value of a put option is the reverse: the maximum of $X - S_0$ or zero, whichever is larger. For a put, the option is in the money if $X - S_0$ is positive; otherwise, the intrinsic value of the put option is zero.

The difference, or residual, between the total market price of the option and the current intrinsic value is the time value component of the option. As shown in Figure 4.2, the time value component of the option price is a function of the underlying security's expected volatility, $\sigma$, the current level of interest rates, $r$, and the option's maturity date or time to expiration, $T$. The term *time value* comes from the fact that this component of the total option price gradually approaches zero as the option nears expiration, leaving only the intrinsic value. The convergence of the total option price to the intrinsic value component at expiration is similar to the convergence of a futures contract price to the underlying security price at expiration.

We will use some option prices for Apple Inc. (ticker AAPL) to illustrate these concepts. Consider the call and put option prices on Tuesday, 22 March 2012, when AAPL was trading for $614.50 per share. **Table 4.1** lists the call

**Table 4.1.    AAPL Stock Option Prices on 22 March 2012**

| April Expiration | | | August Expiration | | |
|---|---|---|---|---|---|
| Strike | Call | Put | Strike | Call | Put |
| 605 | 23.45 | 13.90 | 605 | 53.50 | 43.00 |
| 610 | 20.75 | 16.15 | 610 | 51.05 | 45.55 |
| 615 | 18.20 | 18.60 | 615 | 48.70 | 48.20 |
| 620 | 15.90 | 20.30 | 620 | 46.45 | 50.95 |
| 625 | 13.85 | 24.25 | 625 | 44.25 | 53.75 |

and put option prices for five strike prices and two expiration dates, 20 April and 17 August. The first expiration date is about one month away from the March date, and the second expiration date is about five months away. The quotes in Table 4.1 illustrate several important properties of American-style option prices.

- *A call option should be worth at least as much as its intrinsic value.* This property is best illustrated with an in-the-money option. For example, the April expiration 610-strike-price call is in the money with an intrinsic value of 614.50 − 610 = $4.50, whereas the total price of the option is $20.75. Thus, the time value component of this option is 20.75 − 4.50 = $16.25, well above zero. In fact, given that the intrinsic value is zero for the options that are currently out of the money, all of the option prices listed in Table 4.1 exceed the option's intrinsic value.

- *Call options having the same maturity but with higher strike prices are more out of the money and thus are worth less.* The logic of this characteristic is that a larger (but less likely) move in the stock price will be needed for the option with the higher strike price to pay off. For example, the price of the April expiration 615 call, which is slightly out of the money, is $18.20, compared with the 610 call price of $20.75. In fact, the call prices all decline with each increase in strike price for both April and August expirations in Table 4.1.

- *Call options having the same strike price but with longer maturities are more valuable than those with shorter maturities.* In other words, the time value increases with maturity. For example, the price of the August expiration 610 strike-price call is $51.05 with a time value component of 51.05 − 4.50 = $46.55, compared with the $20.75 price of the corresponding April expiration call option. In fact, the August expiration option price is higher than the corresponding April expiration price for all of the call options in Table 4.1.

The price of a generic call option as a function of the underlying asset price is illustrated in **Figure 4.3**. Notice that the call price (black line) increases as the asset price increases and that the intrinsic value (dotted line) is zero until the asset price exceeds the strike price of the option, *X*. For underlying security prices above the strike price, the intrinsic value increases dollar for dollar with the underlying asset price. The time value component (vertical distance *between* the black and dotted lines) reaches a maximum value at the option strike price and then declines toward zero as the call option goes further in the money.

As shown in Table 4.1, American-style put option prices have similar properties to call option prices:

- *A put option should be worth at least as much as its intrinsic value.* For example, the April expiration 610-strike-price option is out of the money because 610 is less than \$614.40 and thus has a zero intrinsic value, but the option price is still positive at \$15.15. Like with call options, the put options' market prices listed in Table 4.1 all exceed the intrinsic value component.

- *Put options having the same maturity but with higher strike prices are more in the money and thus are worth more.* For example, the slightly in-the-money 615-strike-price put option, which has an intrinsic value of 615 − 614.50 = \$0.50, has a higher price at \$18.60 than the 610-strike-price put. In fact,

**Figure 4.3.    Value of a Call Option**

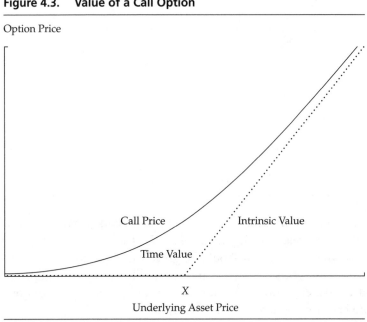

the total option price increases with each increase in the strike price for all the put options in Table 4.1.

• *Like call options, put options having the same strike price but with longer maturities are more valuable than those with shorter maturities.* For example, the price of the 610-strike-price put option for August expiration is $45.55, quite a bit higher than the $16.15 price of the corresponding April expiration put option.

**Figure 4.4** illustrates the value of a generic put option (black line) as a function of the underlying asset price, together with its intrinsic value and time value. As with the call option in Figure 4.3, the intrinsic value component of the put option price is a kinked but piece-wise linear function of the underlying asset price, whereas the time value component (vertical distance between the black and dotted lines) reaches its maximum value at the option exercise price.

**Figure 4.4.   Value of a Put Option**

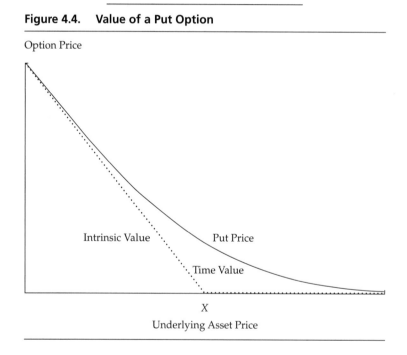

The option-pricing properties we have discussed so far are summarized by the algebraic relationships in **Table 4.2**. The last entry notes that the price of an American option should be greater than or equal to the price of a European option with the same parameters. This property follows from the fact that an American option can do everything a European option can do and more because it can be exercised early.

**Table 4.2. American Option-Pricing Relationships**

|  | Call Option ($C$) | Put Option ($P$) |
|---|---|---|
| Minimum option price, intrinsic value | $\max(0, S_0 - X)$ | $\max(0, X - S_0)$ |
| Impact of exercise price ($X_1 < X_2$) | $C(X_1) \geq C(X_2)$ | $P(X_1) \leq P(X_2)$ |
| Impact of time to expiration ($T_1 < T_2$) | $C(T_1) \leq C(T_2)$ | $P(T_1) \leq P(T_2)$ |
| Early exercise | American $\geq$ European option prices | |

Several other properties of option prices will be explored in Chapter 5, but we note an additional one here: *The percentage change in an option price is typically much larger than the corresponding change in the underlying asset price.* This so-called implicit leverage is part of what makes options useful for hedging risk in the underlying asset. But it also means that the value of the option is quite volatile when held by itself, particularly in the case of out-of-the money options. For example, the April expiration 620 strike-call option in Table 4.1 has a price of $15.90, based on the underlying Apple stock price of $614.50. Suppose an investor bought this option in anticipation of a price rise in Apple shares but then the share price dropped the next day to $600. The fair price for this option at the new lower stock price, assuming no change in the expected volatility of the stock, turns out to be about $10.00. Thus, the percentage price drop in AAPL shares is only 600/614.50 − 1 = −2.36%, a small loss. But the return for the option investor is $10.00/$15.90 − 1 = −37.1%, a much more substantial loss. Indeed, the magnitude of the loss in the option contract represents a leverage factor of about 16 to 1 (i.e., 37.11/2.36), much more leverage than an individual investor could obtain by buying the stock on margin (i.e., 2 to 1). This kind of price volatility with options is the rule rather than the exception and entails substantially more volatility than do positions in the underlying asset.

More insight into the characteristics of options can be obtained by examining their *payoff* values at expiration. The *contingency table* is one technique for showing the expiration value of various option positions and strategies. In the following table, we show the individual values of a long call, a long put, and the underlying security—*contingent on* whether the price of security $S_T$ is above or below the exercise price on the option expiration date.

|  | $S_T < X$ | $S_T > X$ |
|---|---|---|
| Call option | 0 | $S_T - X$ |
| Put option | $X - S_T$ | 0 |
| Security | $S_T$ | $S_T$ |

In the first row, the call option has value at expiration if and only if the underlying asset price is above the strike price, $X$. In the second row, the put option has value at expiration if and only if the underlying asset price is below the strike price, $X$. In the third row, the value of the underlying security, $S_T$, is the same whether it is below or above the option's exercise price. As the reader will see, contingency tables can be expanded to include writing (short selling) options and various combinations of options and the underlying security.

Another useful tool for option analysis is a *hockey stick* diagram of the expiration date payoff as a function of the underlying asset price. For example, **Figure 4.5** illustrates the payoff pattern for a call option at expiration. The horizontal axis is the underlying security price and the vertical axis measures the gross payoff (solid line) and net payoff (dotted line) of the call option. The net payoff equals the gross payoff minus the price the investor pays initially to acquire the option, $C$.

On the one hand, if the security price ends up below the strike price, $X$, the gross payoff to the call option is zero, as shown on the left side of Figure 4.5. On the other hand, if the security price ends up above the exercise price, the gross payoff to the call option is the difference between the security price and the strike price, $S_T - X$, as shown on the right side of Figure 4.5.

**Figure 4.5.  Payoff Profile of a Call Option**

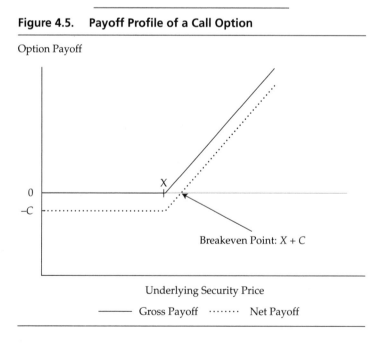

©2013 The Research Foundation of CFA Institute

The net payoff from the call option is a constant negative value until the security price reaches the exercise price. From that point, the net payoff (dotted line) starts to rise. The investor breaks even, with zero net profit, at the point where the security price equals the strike price plus the initial price paid for the option. The investor enjoys a positive net profit if the underlying asset price ends up greater than the breakeven point. Note that the call option payoff has a kinked or asymmetrical payoff pattern, which distinguishes it from a futures contract. As the reader will see, this asymmetry in the payoff allows the option to create specialized return patterns at expiration that are unavailable when using a futures contract.

**Figure 4.6** is the payoff diagram for a put option. The put option has a gross payoff of zero if the underlying security price ends up above the exercise price, as shown on the right side of the figure. If the underlying asset price is below the strike price, the gross payoff to the put option is $X - S_T$, with the maximum gross payoff being $X$ if the underlying security price goes all the way to zero. The net payoff is shown by the dotted line, which is shifted down from the gross payoff by the initial cost of the put option, $P$. The investor breaks even, with zero net profit, at the point where the security price equals the strike price minus the initial price of the put option. The investor in a put option incurs a net loss if the security price is above that value at the expiration of the option.

**Figure 4.6. Payoff Profile of a Put Option**

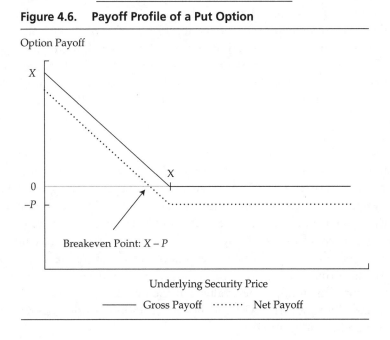

## Option Strategies

The payoff profiles for buying call and put options, together with the payoff profiles for selling options, can be used to understand common option strategies. These strategies include covered calls, protective puts, and more complicated option strategies, such as straddles and option spreads. Illustrations of other common strategies are contained in the exercises section at the end of this book.

**Covered Call.** An investor constructs a covered call position by selling a call option on shares of an underlying security that is already owned. The following contingency table shows how the value of a covered call depends on the price of the underlying security at the expiration date:

|  | $S_T < X$ | $S_T > X$ |
|---|---|---|
| Security | $S_T$ | $S_T$ |
| – Call option | 0 | $-(S_T - X)$ |
| Total payoff | $\bar{S}_T$ | $\overline{X}$ |

The first row of the table shows that the underlying security has a value of $S_T$ at the expiration of the option, independent of whether that price is above or below the option's exercise price. The second row shows that the call option has a value of zero if the underlying security price ends up below the option's exercise price. If the underlying security is above the exercise price of the call, then the option expires in the money with a value of $S_T - X$. Because the call option has been sold instead of purchased, the payoff requires a negative sign. Totaling up the columns provides the gross payoff when the security is either below or above the exercise price at expiration. Specifically, if the security price is below the exercise price, the covered call position is worth $S_T$, and if the security price is above the exercise price, the covered call position is worth $X$.

**Figure 4.7** illustrates the gross payoff for the covered call, with a dotted line added for the net payoff, which includes the price received for the call option that is written or sold. As shown on the diagram, the gross payoff to the covered call position represented by the heavy solid line is $S_T$ until the underlying security reaches a price of $X$. For underlying security prices above $X$, the gross payoff to the covered call is capped at $X$ no matter how high the price goes. The dotted line represents the total covered call value when the premium that was received by selling the call option, $C$, is also taken into account. This total, or net, value can then be compared with the payoff on the underlying security without the added option position, shown by the lighter solid line in Figure 4.7.

**Figure 4.7.  Payoff Profile of a Covered Call**

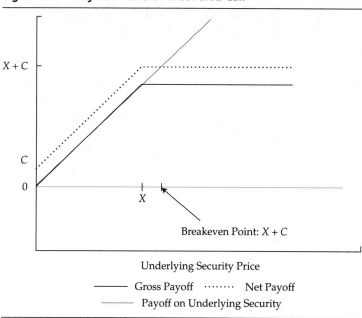

Underlying Security Price

——— Gross Payoff   ········ Net Payoff
------- Payoff on Underlying Security

The benefit of the covered call occurs when the underlying security price is below the exercise price, in which the total value (dotted line) is consistently a little higher than the value of the security itself. The risk of the strategy lies above the strike price, in which the covered call does not fully participate in the market rise. The breakeven point, or net payoff of zero, occurs when the security price equals the strike price plus the original price of the call option. Thus, the covered call is not a "free lunch" because there are ending security prices for which the investor is worse off for having written the covered call.

**Protective Put.** A protective put is constructed by buying a put option, typically out of the money, on a security that the investor already owns. The contingency table for the protective put follows.

|  | $S_T < X$ | $S_T > X$ |
|---|---|---|
| Security | $S_T$ | $S_T$ |
| Put option | $X - S_T$ | 0 |
| Total payoff | $\overline{X}$ | $\overline{S_T}$ |

The first row of the contingency table shows that the value of the security is $S_T$ whether it ends up being above or below the exercise price on the expiration date. In the second row, the value of the put option is $X - S_T$ below the option's exercise price and is zero above the exercise price. The total gross payoff of the protective put strategy is found by adding up the value in each column, so the protective put is worth $X$ below the exercise price and $S_T$ above the exercise price.

The protective put is depicted graphically in **Figure 4.8**. The light solid line represents the security value in isolation, and the heavier solid line represents the gross payoff to the put option and the security combined. Below the exercise price, the put option compensates for the lower security price, so the total gross payoff is constant at a value of $X$. Once the original cost of the put option is accounted for, the net payoff is represented by the dotted line. The breakeven point, or zero net profit, on the protective put occurs when the security price is equal to the strike price minus the cost of the put option.

**Figure 4.8.   Payoff Profile of a Protective Put**

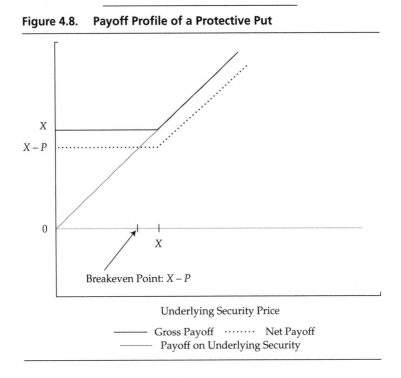

Underlying Security Price

——— Gross Payoff   ········ Net Payoff
——— Payoff on Underlying Security

As shown in Figure 4.8, the benefit of the protective put occurs below the exercise price, where the combination of security and put option is worth more than the security itself, thus putting a floor on the value of the combined package. The option market does not give this downside protection for free, however, in that above the exercise price, the net value of the protected put is worth a little bit less than the security. The protective put is sometimes known as *portfolio insurance* because the put option protects the value if the security price falls while maintaining some market exposure if the price rises.

**Straddle.** The straddle is an option strategy that involves the purchase of both a put and a call at a given exercise price but does not include a position in the underlying security. The contingency table for the straddle follows.

|  | $S_T < X$ | $S_T > X$ |
|---|---|---|
| Call option | 0 | $S_T - X$ |
| Put option | $X - S_T$ | 0 |
| Total payoff | $X - S_T$ | $S_T - X$ |

The call option in the first row has a value of zero below $X$ and a value of $S_T - X$ above $X$. The put option in the second row has a value of $X - S_T$ below $X$ and a value of zero above $X$. The total gross payoff shown in the bottom row is thus $X - S_T$ below $X$ and $S_T - X$ above $X$.

The net payoff for the straddle is illustrated by the dotted line in **Figure 4.9**. The breakeven points for this strategy incorporate the cost of both the call and put options and are positioned on either side of the strike price. The investor enjoys a positive profit if the security price moves away from the strike price and falls outside the breakeven points. In other

**Figure 4.9.   Payoff Profile of a Straddle**

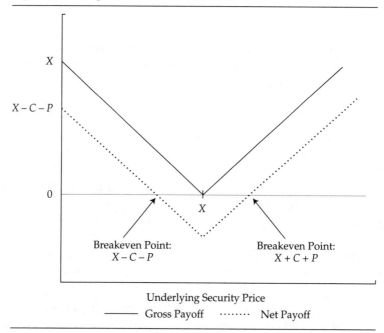

Underlying Security Price

——— Gross Payoff    ········ Net Payoff

words, if the security price makes a big move up or down, the investor makes money, but the investor loses money if the underlying security price stays relatively constant.

A straddle can be used when the investor is uncertain about the direction of a price change in the underlying security but believes that a large change will occur. As we will discuss in Chapter 5 on option pricing, the straddle actually makes money, net of the cost of the option, if the underlying asset price moves *more* than the volatility estimated by other participants in the market, as embedded in the option's time value component.

**Bull Call Spread.** The bull call spread is constructed by buying a call option with an exercise price of $X_1$ and simultaneously selling a call option with a higher exercise price of $X_2$. The bull call spread is more complex than the previous strategies because the position involves more than one strike price. Because the investor needs to know how the spread will behave above and below each strike price, the contingency table must be enlarged into three columns. The contingency table for the bull call spread follows.

|  | $S_T < X_1$ | $X_1 < S_T < X_2$ | $S_T > X_2$ |
|---|---|---|---|
| Call option #1 | 0 | $S_T - X_1$ | $S_T - X_1$ |
| – Call option #2 | 0 | 0 | $-(S_T - X_2)$ |
| Total payoff | $\overline{0}$ | $\overline{S_T - X_1}$ | $\overline{X_2 - X_1}$ |

The first row shows that the call option with the lower strike price, $X_1$, has no value when the underlying security falls below that value. But for underlying security prices that are greater than $X_1$, this call option is in the money and has a value of $S_T - X_1$, independent of whether the security price is above $X_2$. The second row in the table shows that the call option sold has no value as long as the underlying security price is less than $X_2$. When the security price is greater than $X_2$, the payoff for this option is $-(S_T - X_2)$, where the minus sign in front of the term indicates this option has been sold. In the last row, we see that the total payoff at expiration is zero when the security price is below $X_1$, is $S_T - X_1$ when the security price is between $X_1$ and $X_2$, and is $X_2 - X_1$ when the underlying security price is above $X_2$.

The gross and net payoffs to the bull call spread are illustrated graphically in **Figure 4.10**. Until the security price reaches $X_1$, the gross payoff is zero. Above $X_2$, the gross payoff is $X_2 - X_1$. Between $X_2$ and $X_1$, the gross payoff is a diagonal line connecting the two. The dotted line in Figure 4.10 shows the net payoff that accounts for the cost of the option bought as well as the price

**Figure 4.10. Payoff Profile of a Bull Call Spread**

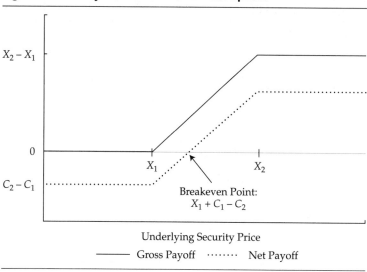

Underlying Security Price

——— Gross Payoff ⋯⋯⋯ Net Payoff

received for the option sold. The breakeven or zero net profit point for the bull call spread is where the security price equals the lower strike price, $X_1$, plus the net cost of the two call options, $C_1 - C_2$. $C_1$ will be more expensive than $C_2$ because it has a lower exercise price. Thus, loss is limited if the security price declines, but the gain is also limited if the security price goes up. This option spread is "bullish" in the sense that the higher payoffs occur when the security price has gone up.

**Pre-Expiration-Date Analysis.** To this point in the chapter, we have examined option strategies from the perspective of their terminal value at the expiration date. Specifically, both the contingency tables and the payoff diagrams have been based on the combined value of the separate elements at the expiration date of the options that are used. Although somewhat simplistic, these techniques are popular because they allow the investor to easily keep track of all the individual pieces of the strategy as well as their combined effect. But many strategies are not held to the expiration date of the options, so some attention to the pre-expiration-date payoff is also warranted. Drawing profiles of pre-expiration-date payoffs requires the use of a pricing model to value the option positions at a point in time prior to expiration, a topic we explore in Chapter 5. For example, **Figure 4.11** illustrates the profit profile of the bull call spread prior to the expiration of the options. Note that the sharp corners of the payoff profile are smoothed in comparison with Figure 4.10. As the time to expiration draws near, the profile becomes sharper and closer to the expiration date shape shown in Figure 4.10.

**Figure 4.11. Net Payoff Profile of a Bull Call Spread before Expiration**

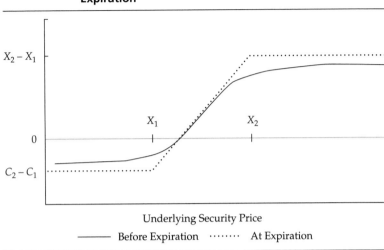

## Choosing a Strategy

The choice of an option strategy depends on at least two investor perspectives—on the direction (up or down) of the price change for the underlying security and on the cost (cheap or expensive) of the options. **Figure 4.12** shows how these two perspectives inform the type of option (put or call) in which the investor might take a position and whether to buy or sell them.

First, on the vertical axis, when an investor is bullish on the underlying security, the best strategies generally involve buying call options and/or selling put options. When the investor is bearish on the underlying security, the best strategies generally involve buying puts and/or selling calls.

The second dimension relates to the cost of the options, which under arbitrage-free pricing comes down to the investor's belief about the volatility of the underlying security. On the one hand, if the investor believes the actual volatility of the underlying security will be low relative to market expectations, then the options will seem expensive and the investor will generally want to sell rather than buy them. On the other hand, if the investor believes the actual volatility of the underlying security will be high relative to market expectations, then the options will seem cheap and the investor will generally want to buy rather than sell them. For example, if the investor is bearish and the options are not expensive, buying put options outright or using a protected put strategy with the underlying security is attractive. If the investor is neutral in terms of market direction and the options are expensive, selling a straddle (selling both a put and a call) or taking other kinds of "short volatility" positions can be attractive. Thus, expectations of both the direction and the volatility in the underlying security help investors establish a framework within which to develop option strategies.

**Figure 4.12.  Option Strategies: Perspective on Market Direction and Option Price**

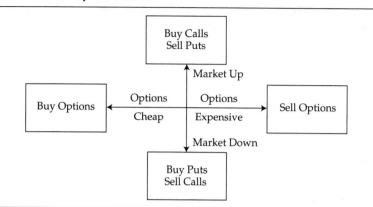

The choice of strike prices on the options and the choice of option maturity also come into play, but the two most important considerations relate to the investor's view on the direction of change in the underlying security price and the investor's view on volatility. Specifically, given general informational efficiency of financial markets, what really matters is the investor's view on the value and volatility of the underlying security relative to the view of other market participants. In Chapter 5, we develop tools to determine the volatility of the underlying security that is implied by any given option price.

## Probability Distribution of Returns

The contingency tables and payoff diagrams we have used to this point provide perspective on the range of potential payoffs to various option strategies but do not account for the probability of any specific payoff actually occurring. For example, in accordance with a typical bell-shaped probability distribution, small changes in the underlying security price between the time an option is purchased and the time it is sold are clearly more likely than large price moves. The probability distribution of returns to an option strategy depends not only on the probability distribution of the underlying security but also on the configuration of options selected.

For example, consider the covered call strategy of selling call options on an individual security that the investor already owns. The solid line in **Figure 4.13** shows a typical lognormal probability distribution of one-month returns on an individual stock, with a mean return of 1% and standard deviation of 10%. The dotted line shows how the probability distribution is affected by selling call options that are 10% out of the money to cover 50% of the underlying security position. The light solid line shows the impact of selling enough call options to cover 100% of the security positions. Note how the shape of the probability

**Figure 4.13.    Probability Distribution for a Covered Call**

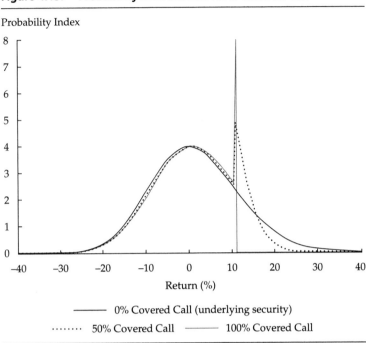

Probability Index

0% Covered Call (underlying security)

········  50% Covered Call  ———— 100% Covered Call

distribution changes as an increasing proportion of call options are sold relative to the underlying security position. Selling call options draws the return distribution back on the right side, thus increasing the chance that an investor will receive only moderate returns. The light solid curve shows that selling call options on 100% of the underlying security position completely truncates the right side of the probability distribution at 11%, based on the 10% out-of-the-money strike price plus an additional 1% return from the proceeds of selling the call.

**Figure 4.14** illustrates how the probability distribution is affected by buying protective puts that are 5% out of the money. Buying put options on 50% of the underlying security position truncates the left side of the probability distribution and increases the probability of moderate returns. On the right side of the distribution, the cost of the protective put is evidenced by a slightly lower probability of achieving any particular return, in that the dotted line is slightly below the dark solid line. Figure 4.14 also shows that purchasing protective puts on 100% of the security portfolio completely truncates the left side of the distribution at –7%, based on the –5% strike price of the put options minus 2 additional percentage points of total return for the cost of the options.

**Figure 4.15** illustrates the effect of simultaneously selling call options and buying put options on an underlying stock position, where in this example the cost of the puts slightly exceeds the proceeds from selling the calls. The

**Figure 4.14.  Probability Distribution for a Protective Put**

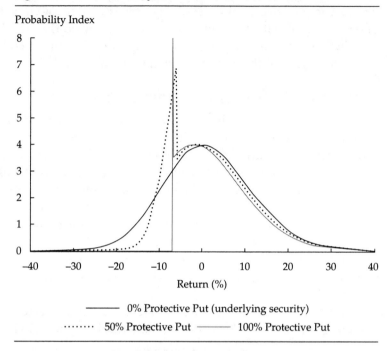

**Figure 4.15.  Distribution for a Protective Put and Covered Call**

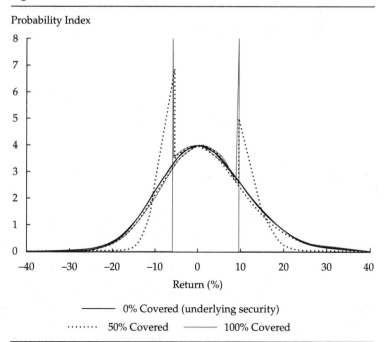

combination causes a truncation of the return probability distribution in both tails. The key concept revealed by these diagrams is that the asymmetrical nature of option payoffs allows an investor to shape and mold the probability distribution by truncating some parts and adding to others. In general, call options affect the right tail the most and put options affect the left tail.

## Mean–Variance Performance Comparisons

Common performance metrics in portfolio management depend on the expected return and risk of a strategy, where risk is measured by the variance or standard deviation of return. In general, such tools as risk–return diagrams and Sharpe ratios are less pertinent to option strategies because of the highly skewed nature of the probability distributions. For example, the probability distribution for the underlying security in Figure 4.14 is generally symmetrical, indicative of a one-month return on a common stock. The probability distribution for the full protective put strategy in Figure 4.14, however, is highly asymmetrical, so standard deviation does not tell the whole story. As a result, the familiar risk–return diagrams from mean–variance portfolio theory do not give a complete picture of option strategies.

For an illustration, consider the diagram for one-month expected return versus risk in **Figure 4.16**. The slope of the straight line in Figure 4.16 is based

**Figure 4.16.    Risk–Return Tradeoffs for Option Positions**

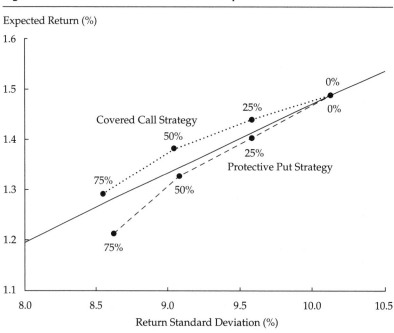

on the Sharpe ratio of the underlying stock without any modifications for option strategies. As the covered call strategy shown in Figure 4.13 is used, the expected return and risk decline—but not in a linear fashion. For example, the 50% covered call strategy appears to have a superior risk–return position than the completely unhedged (0% covered call) position. The protective put strategy in Figure 4.14 appears to have an inferior risk–return tradeoff. But both perspectives are misleading because of the highly asymmetrical nature of the probability distributions shown in Figure 4.13 and Figure 4.14, which are not completely captured by standard deviation.

As the reader will see in Chapter 5, the expected return to a fairly priced option is simply some multiple of the expected return on the underlying security. For example, the short-term expected excess return for buying a call option might be five times the expected excess return on the underlying stock. Thus, the mean or expected return on options simply reflects basic leverage on long and short positions in the underlying security and is not the problem. The problem is that measuring risk by standard deviation, as in the denominator of the Sharpe ratio, provides an incomplete perspective on risk. Adequate perspective on the risk of option-based strategies requires an examination of the entire probability distribution of returns in either graphic or tabular form.

For example, **Table 4.3** shows the probability of returns falling in various ranges for the underlying stock and for the 100% covered call and protective put strategies illustrated in Figures 4.13 and 4.14. As shown in Table 4.3, the covered call strategy has a high probability of moderate returns in the

**Table 4.3   Comparison of Return Range Probability**

| Percentage Return Range | Underlying Stock | Covered Call | Protective Put |
|---|---|---|---|
| Below –25 | 0.1% | 0.0% | 0.0% |
| –25 to –20 | 0.9 | 0.2% | 0.0 |
| –20 to –15 | 3.3 | 0.8 | 0.0 |
| –15 to –10 | 8.3 | 2.3 | 0.0 |
| –10 to –5 | 14.6 | 4.3 | 82.7 |
| –5 to 0 | 19.1 | 6.0 | 5.2 |
| 0 to +5 | 19.1 | 6.3 | 4.7 |
| +5 to +10 | 15.2 | 5.2 | 3.5 |
| +10 to +15 | 9.9 | 74.9 | 2.1 |
| +15 to +20 | 5.4 | 0.0 | 1.1 |
| +20 to +25 | 2.6 | 0.0 | 0.5 |
| Above +25 | 1.6 | 0.0 | 0.3 |
| Total | 100.0% | 100.0% | 100.0% |

+10% to +15% range but no probability of larger returns. But the protective put strategy has no probability of returns below –10% and preserves some probability of high returns. Like the probability distribution diagrams themselves, the tabulation of the range of return probabilities gives some idea of what tradeoffs are being made in the strategies, but the investor must still decide which tradeoffs are preferred. To summarize, option strategies cause distortions to standard symmetrical return distributions that are large enough to make mean–variance comparisons erroneous.

# 5. Option Contracts: Pricing Relationships

Options are derivative securities, so the price of an option depends on the value of the underlying security, but it also depends on several other factors. We explore a number of arbitrage-based relationships and then introduce formal option valuation methodologies, including binomial pricing and the Black–Scholes model. Profitable strategies that are essentially risk free restrict the price of options within specific bounds. Thus, the market price of an option contract, similar to that of a futures contract, is ultimately driven by the principle of arbitrage. As we noted in discussing futures contracts, the arbitrage-based price of an option is not directly dependent on the expected future price of the underlying security, only indirectly as reflected in the current price of the underlying security.

## Lower-Bound Adjustments for Put and Call Options

In this section, we will distinguish between the prices of American options, $C_0$ and $P_0$ (upper case), and the prices of European options, $c_0$ and $p_0$ (lower case). In Chapter 4, we explained why the price of an American option should at least be equal to its intrinsic or exercise value, specifically $C_0 \geq S_0 - X$, where $S_0$ is the current price and $X$ is the exercise price of the option. In fact, the minimum price boundary for an American call is a bit higher than that.

To derive the higher boundary, consider the strategy of buying a European call and simultaneously investing in cash amounting to

$$\frac{X}{(1+r)^T} + D,$$

where $r$ is a risk-free annualized rate and $D$ is the present value of any dividends paid by the security before option expiration at time $T$. The contingency table for the payoff at expiration to this portfolio follows.

| | $S_T < X$ | $S_T > X$ |
|---|---|---|
| European call option | 0 | $S_T - X$ |
| Cash $= X/(1+r)^T + D$ | $X + D(1+r)^T$ | $X + D(1+r)^T$ |
| Total payoff | $X + D(1+r)^T$ | $S_T + D(1+r)^T$ |

As shown in the bottom row, the total payoff under either contingency is equal to or greater than the value of the underlying security together with dividends at expiration. Thus, the initial price for establishing the portfolio must be greater than the initial price of the underlying security,

$$c_0 + \frac{X}{(1+r)^T} + D > S_0. \qquad (5.1)$$

Rearranging terms in Equation 5.1, we have a minimum price limit for the European call option:

$$c_0 > (S_0 - X) + \left( X - \frac{X}{(1+r)^T} \right) - D. \qquad (5.2)$$

The last part of Equation 5.2 shows that if we disregard any dividends, the European call option will always be worth more than its intrinsic value, $S_0 - X$. Because an American option is always worth at least as much as a European option, this condition must also be true for an American call option. But with a large enough dividend, the European call option could be worth less than its intrinsic value without any way to capture the intrinsic value by early exercise.

If we define the time value of an option to be equal to the difference between the option price and the intrinsic value, we can write the time value for a call option using Equation 5.2 as

$$c_0 - (S_0 - X) = \left[ X - \frac{X}{(1+r)^T} \right] - D + I_c, \qquad (5.3)$$

where the term in brackets represents the interest opportunity cost of the exercise price between now and the expiration of the option. We use $I_c$ to represent the "insurance value" of the call option in order to make Equation 5.2 an equality. The insurance value comes from the fact that a call option benefits if the price of the security moves up but the loss is limited if the security moves down. Unless expected cash distributions are large relative to the interest opportunity cost and the insurance value, the time value will be positive.

For a numerical illustration, consider the following parameters for a European call:

| | | |
|---|---|---|
| $S_0 = \$105$ | $X = \$100$ | $r = 1.8\%$ |
| $T = 1/12$ (one month) | $c_0 = \$7.75$ | $D = \$0$ |

The intrinsic value component of this call option is $105 - 100 = \$5.00$, so the time value component of the $7.75 total price is $2.75. The time value component of $2.75 can be further decomposed into an interest opportunity cost of 15 cents,

$$X - \frac{X}{(1+r)^T} = \$100 - \frac{\$100}{(1+0.018)^{1/12}} = \$0.15,$$

and the remaining insurance value of the call, $I_c = \$2.60$.

To examine a similar lower bound for a put option, consider the contingency table for a portfolio composed of a European put option and the security.

|  | $S_T < X$ | $S_T > X$ |
|---|---|---|
| European put option | $X - S_T$ | 0 |
| Security | $S_T + D(1+r)^T$ | $S_T + D(1+r)^T$ |
| Total payoff | $X + D(1+r)^T$ | $S_T + D(1+r)^T$ |

The portfolio payoff under either contingency is greater than or equal to the exercise price and the future value of dividends, so the current portfolio value must be worth more than the present value of the exercise price and the dividends:

$$p_0 + S_0 > \frac{X}{(1+r)^T} + D. \tag{5.4}$$

Rearranging terms in Equation 5.4 gives us a minimum price limit for the European put option as

$$p_0 > (X - S_0) + D - \left[ X - \frac{X}{(1+r)^T} \right]. \tag{5.5}$$

This condition must also be true for an American put option because it is always worth at least as much as a European put option. Depending on the time to maturity and the level of interest rates, the European put option price may or may not be greater than the intrinsic value, $X - S_0$. Indeed, a European put option that is deep in the money may have a negative time value without any way to cash in on the intrinsic value by early exercise.

Using Equation 5.5, we can write the time value of a European put option as

$$p_0 - (X - S_0) = D - \left[ X - \frac{X}{(1+r)^T} \right] + I_p, \tag{5.6}$$

where the term in brackets again represents the interest opportunity cost of the exercise price of the option between now and expiration. The term in brackets is preceded by a negative sign because the potential receipt of the exercise price earlier rather than later allows the investor to earn interest on that amount. We use $I_p$ to represent the insurance value of the put option in order to make Equation 5.5 an equality. The insurance value comes from the fact that the put option benefits if the price of the security moves down but the loss is limited if the security moves up.

To illustrate, suppose the underlying security in the preceding example dropped from \$105 all the way down to \$80. Now, the pricing parameters are

| $S_0 = \$80$ | $X = \$100$ | $r = 1.8\%$ |
|---|---|---|
| $T = 1/12$ (one month) | $D = \$0$ | $p_0 = \$19.95$ |

At an underlying security price of $80, the intrinsic value of the put option is $100 - 80 = \$20.00$, so the time value component is $-\$0.05$, or negative five cents. Specifically, the time value component of the European put price is composed of $-\$0.15$ of interest opportunity cost plus the insurance value of the put option, $0.10. This example shows that the time value might actually be negative for the put option if it cannot be exercised early. We will examine the possibility of early exercise for deep in-the-money puts later in this chapter.

## Put–Call Parity for European Options

Another important pricing restriction, specific to European options, is the arbitrage relationship known as *put–call parity*. To understand this relationship, consider a portfolio composed of buying the underlying security, buying a European put option on that security, and simultaneously selling a European call option with the same expiration date and strike price. The contingency table follows.

|  | $S_T < X$ | $S_T > X$ |
|---|---|---|
| Security | $S_T + D(1 + r)^T$ | $S_T + D(1 + r)^T$ |
| European put option | $X - S_T$ | 0 |
| – European call option | 0 | $-(S_T - X)$ |
| Total payoff | $X + D(1 + r)^T$ | $X + D(1 + r)^T$ |

The total payoff to this portfolio at expiration is $X + D(1 + r)^T$, no matter what the security price is at time $T$. Because the payoff is certain, the upfront cost of this portfolio at Time 0 must be the present value of $X$ based on a risk-free rate, $r$, plus dividends, or

$$\frac{X}{(1+r)^T} + D = S_0 + p_0 - c_0. \tag{5.7}$$

Note that the relationship in this arbitrage argument is a strict equality, not simply a minimum or maximum limit on option prices. Rearranging the terms in Equation 5.7 gives the spread between the current price of a European call option and a European put with the same strike price and expiration date as

$$c_0 - p_0 = S_0 - D - \frac{X}{(1+r)^T}. \tag{5.8}$$

The relationship involves the price of the underlying security, the present value of any dividends to be paid before expiration, and the present value of $X$.

As the reader will see later on, one can rearrange this put–call parity relationship in various ways for additional insights. Strictly speaking, this arbitrage relationship holds only for European put–call pairs. If this relationship did not hold, then one could create greater-than-riskless returns without any risk by selling the expensive combination of assets and buying the cheap combination. Thus, put–call parity is analogous to the cash-and-carry arbitrage condition for futures contracts, also known as spot–futures parity.

## Early Exercise of American Options

By contract specification, American options can be exercised early. Although early exercise is generally not desirable, there are notable exceptions. Specifically, investors who want to terminate an option position early will typically receive more money from selling the option than from exercising it. The fact that the current market price of the option generally exceeds its intrinsic value leads to the saying that the option is "worth more alive than dead."

The lower bound for the price of an American call option was suggested in Equation 5.2 as

$$c_0 > (S_0 - X) + \left[ X - \frac{X}{(1+r)^T} \right] - D. \tag{5.9}$$

Assuming for a moment that no dividends are expected before expiration ($D = 0$), the price of the American call option must be greater than the intrinsic value, $S_0 - X$, because for a positive interest rate, $X$ is greater than $X/(1 + r)^T$. In other words, without any expected dividends, there is no incentive to exercise the American call option early because selling the option to someone else gives the investor greater value than exercising it and receiving only the intrinsic value. Early exercise of an in-the-money call option may be desirable, however, just before a relatively large cash distribution on the underlying security. Individual stock options in the United States are not dividend protected, meaning that the strike price does not automatically adjust for the natural drop in stock price on the ex-dividend date.

We can gain some insight into possible early exercise of an in-the-money American call option when dividends are expected by using the put–call parity relationship in Equation 5.8. Rearranging the European put–call parity relationship gives

$$(S_0 - X) - c_0 = D - \left[ X - \frac{X}{(1+r)^T} \right] - p_0. \tag{5.10}$$

The intrinsic value of a European call option, $S_0 - X$, will exceed the European call price, $c_0$, if $D > X - X/(1 + r)^T + p_0$. If the expected dividend is large enough, it might be desirable to exercise the option in order to capture the intrinsic value. In other words, early exercise of a call option may be optimal if a pending dividend on the underlying stock exceeds the time value component, composed of the interest opportunity cost, $X - X/(1 + r)^T$, and the price of a European put option. This statement suggests the possibility of desirable early exercise, but it is only an approximation because we have used European options, not American options, to derive the insight.

For example, the numerical illustration in the preceding section started with a call option that was $5 in the money. The call option price was $7.75, with an exercise value of $5.00 and a time value component of $2.75. The time value included an interest opportunity cost of $0.15 and an insurance value of the call option (approximated by the price of a European put option) of $2.60.

Thus, if this stock were going to pay a cash dividend of $2.75 per share or higher, early exercise of the call option might be optimal just before the ex-dividend date. Intuitively, the dividend needed to trigger the early exercise of a call option needs to be higher if prevailing interest rates are higher. For example, if the interest rate were 5.0% instead of 1.8%, the time value component of the $5 in-the-money call option would be $2.92 instead of $2.75.

We can also gain some insight about the possibility of early exercise for an in-the-money American put option from the put–call parity relationship for European options. Rearranging the relationship in Equation 5.8 gives

$$(X - S_0) - p_0 = \left[ X - \frac{X}{(1+r)^T} \right] - (c_0 + D). \tag{5.11}$$

The exercise value of a put option, $X - S_0$, will exceed the European put price, $p_0$, if $c_0 + D < X - X/(1 + r)^T$. In other words, early exercise of an American put option might be desirable if it is so deeply in the money that a European call option with the same strike price plus the present value of expected dividends is less than the present value of the interest opportunity cost. Again, this statement is only an approximation because we have used European options and not American options to derive the insight.

For example, early exercise would have been profitable in the preceding numerical example for a put option with a strike price of $100 on a stock that had fallen to $80. Specifically, the insurance value of the put option (approximated by the price of a European call option) was worth only $0.10 but the interest opportunity cost on the strike price for one month was $0.15. In fact, sensitivity analysis for a volatility estimate of 40.0% and the Black–Scholes option-pricing formula (to be discussed later in this chapter) show that early put option exercise could be optimal with these parameter values for any stock price below about $81. Of course, given higher interest rates or more time to expiration, the interest opportunity cost would be higher and the put option might not need to be so far in the money. For example, sensitivity analysis shows that if annualized interest rates were at 5.0%, instead of 1.8%, then the breakeven early exercise stock price would be about $85 instead of $81.

We note again that the numerical examples of early exercise of American options have only been approximate because American option prices do not strictly conform to the European put–call parity condition. Specifically, the prices of American options are affected by the *potential* for early exercise even when they are currently out of the money. Our simple analysis suggests that exercising American options early may be advantageous, but the exact timing for early exercise is beyond the scope of the analysis here and generally requires the use of a specific option-pricing model for American options. The important concepts are that (1) it may be desirable to exercise an American call option early if an expected dividend is large and (2) it may be desirable to exercise an American put option early if it is deep enough in the money.

## Put–Call Parity Bounds for American Options

Although the exact put–call parity relationship does not apply to American options, we can use the relationship to derive upper and lower bounds. To derive the lower bound, consider the payoff for a portfolio that contains a European call option, cash equal to $X + D$, shorting the underlying security, and selling an American put. Consider first the case if the American put option is held to expiration. If the put option is not exercised early, the contingency table for the portfolio gives a fixed positive payoff as follows.

|  | $S_T < X$ | $S_T > X$ |
|---|---|---|
| European call option | 0 | $S_T - X$ |
| Cash $= X + D$ | $(X+D)(1+r)^T$ | $(X+D)(1+r)^T$ |
| $-$ Security | $-S_T - D(1+r)^T$ | $-S_T - D(1+r)^T$ |
| $-$ American put option | $-(X - S_T)$ | 0 |
| Total payoff | $X(1+r)^T - X$ | $X(1+r)^T - X$ |

With a fixed total payoff at expiration and a positive interest rate, the initial value of the portfolio would have to be positive to avoid a riskless return with no initial investment:

$$c_0 + X + D - P_0 - S_0 > 0. \tag{5.12}$$

If the American put option is exercised early at some time $t$, the value of the position would be

$$
\begin{aligned}
c_t &+ \left[ (X+D)(1+r)^t - S_t - D_t - (X - S_t) \right] \\
&= c_t + X\left[ (1+r)^T - 1 \right] + \left[ D(1+r)^t - D_t \right],
\end{aligned}
\tag{5.13}
$$

where $c_t$ represents the value of the European call option at time $t$ when the American put is exercised and $D_t$ represents the value of the dividends paid by the security to that point. This payoff would be positive, which suggests that the initial value of the portfolio would also have to be positive whether the put option was exercised early or not.

Rearranging terms in the inequality for the initial portfolio value and using the fact that $C_0 \geq c_0$ gives a lower bound for the difference between the American call and put options:

$$C_0 - P_0 > S_0 - X - D. \tag{5.14}$$

To derive the upper bound for the difference between American call and put options, we begin with the put–call parity relationship for European options as given in Equation 5.8. If no dividends are expected to be paid before expiration, the American call option is worth the same as the European call, $C_0 = c_0$. We also know that the American put option is worth at least as much as the European put, $P_0 \geq p_0$, so with a potentially larger American put price we have

$$C_0(\text{w/o dividends}) - P_0(\text{w/o dividends}) \leq S_0 - \frac{X}{(1+r)^T}. \tag{5.15}$$

With expected dividends, the lower bound for the American call price is smaller, and the lower bound for the put price is larger than without dividends. Consequently, the inequality without dividends will hold even with expected dividends, so the upper bound for the difference between American call and put options with or without expected dividends is

$$C_0 - P_0 \leq S_0 - \frac{X}{(1+r)^T}. \tag{5.16}$$

Therefore, the upper and lower bounds for the American option put–call parity relationship using Equations 5.14 and 5.16 are

$$S_0 - X - D < C_0 - P_0 \leq S_0 - \frac{X}{(1+r)^T}. \tag{5.17}$$

Note, however, that the relationship is not an exact equality as it is for European options.

The pricing relationships for put and call options covered so far in this chapter can be summarized as follows.

| | Call Option | Put Option |
|---|---|---|
| American intrinsic value | $C_0 = \max(0, S_0 - X)$ | $P_0 = \max(0, X - S_0)$ |
| European lower bound | $c_0 > S_0 - X/(1+r)^T - D$ | $p_0 > X/(1+r)^T + D - S_0$ |
| American lower bound | $C_0 \geq c_0$ (equality for $D = 0$) | $P_0 \geq p_0$ |

The put–call parity relationships may be summarized as follows.

| | |
|---|---|
| European put–call parity | $c_0 - p_0 = S_0 - X/(1+r)^T - D$ |
| American put–call parity | $S_0 - X - D < C_0 - P_0 \leq S_0 - X/(1+r)^T$ |

## The Binomial Pricing Model

In the absence of dividends, option prices depend on the price of the underlying security, the strike price, the volatility of the underlying security, the level of interest rates, and time to expiration. Understanding the impact of each of these factors requires a model of the option price, not simply an arbitrage-restricted price range. In this section, we introduce a simple binomial option-pricing argument that will provide a specific price for both call and put options. As with other derivative securities, the pricing logic will be based on an arbitrage relationship between the current price of the option and the underlying security, not a forecast of where the security price will be in the future. Although the single-period binomial pricing example in this section is simple, the reader will see in later sections that the binomial branching logic can be expanded into a more realistic multiperiod setting.

First, consider a call option. Suppose the underlying stock currently has a price of $S_0$ and can only move up to a price of $S_u$ or down to a price of $S_d$ at option expiration. **Figure 5.1** displays the current price and two possible outcomes for the underlying stock and the call option in this simple "binomial

**Figure 5.1. Simple Binomial Pricing Model for a Call Option**

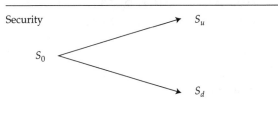

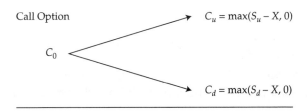

price" world. Assuming that the "up" price of the stock, $S_u$, is higher than the call option exercise price, $X$, the exercise value of the call option if the stock goes up will be

$$C_u = S_u - X. \tag{5.18}$$

If the stock price goes down, the exercise value of the call option, $C_d$, will either be zero or a positive value, $S_d - X$, depending on whether $X$ is above or below the "down" price of the stock, $S_d$.

Now, consider a strategy in which the investor buys the underlying security and simultaneously sells a call option. Specifically, we will buy a fraction, $h_C$, of the underlying stock, so that the upfront price for the strategy is $h_C S_0 - C_0$. The minus sign in front of the current call price acknowledges that the proceeds from *selling* the call option offsets some of the price paid for the underlying stock. If the stock price goes up, the payoff to this strategy will be $h_C S_u - C_u$, and if the stock price goes down, the payoff will be $h_C S_d - C_d$. We want to strategically choose the fraction $h_C$ so that the payoff will be the same no matter which way the stock price moves. Setting the two possible payoffs equal to each other and solving for the hedge ratio, $h_C$, gives

$$h_C = \frac{C_u - C_d}{S_u - S_d}. \tag{5.19}$$

Intuitively, the value of $h_C$ in Equation 5.19 is the range of possible option payoffs divided by the range of possible stock prices and forms a complete hedge. In fact, the hedge ratio $h_C$ given in Equation 5.19 is analogous to the delta of a call option in the Black–Scholes model we discuss later.

Because the payoff to this hedged strategy is the same no matter which way the stock price goes, one could borrow the funds needed to set it up and then use the certain payoff to settle the loan. As a result, the market will force the cost of the strategy to be equal to the present value of the eventual payoff. If the cost were lower, arbitrageurs could borrow money at the risk-free rate and make an easy profit when the payoff occurred. If the cost were higher, arbitrageurs could simply "short" or reverse the positions in the strategy and do the same thing. Thus, arbitrage-free pricing dictates that

$$h_C S_0 - C_0 = \frac{h_C S_u - C_u}{(1+r)^T}$$

and $\hspace{10cm}$ (5.20)

$$h_C S_0 - C_0 = \frac{h_C S_d - C_d}{(1+r)^T}.$$

Note that the value of $h_C$ has been specifically chosen so that the eventual payoff to this strategy is the same whether the stock goes up or down.

Solving for the current price of the call option using either equality in Equation 5.20 gives

$$C_0 = \frac{qC_u + (1-q)C_d}{(1+r)^T},$$

(5.21)

where the new variable $q$ is defined as

$$q = \frac{S_0(1+r)^T - S_d}{S_u - S_d}.$$

(5.22)

Although the value of $C_0$ may be expressed algebraically in a number of ways, Equation 5.21 is particularly useful in understanding the more involved models of option pricing. Specifically, the use of the variable $q$ makes the call price algebraically equivalent to a probability-weighted average of two possible call payoffs, discounted at the risk-free rate. Thus, the variable $q$ is analogous to a "risk-neutral" probability, or the probability that would apply in a world where investors were unconcerned about risk.

For a numerical illustration of single-period binomial option-pricing logic, consider the following set of values. The riskless rate of interest is $r = 5\%$; the time to option expiration is one year, $T = 1$; the current stock price is $S_0 = \$50$; and the strike price of the call option is $X = \$60$. At option expiration, the stock price might go up to $S_u = \$65$ or down to $S_d = \$45$. If the stock price goes up, the call option will expire in the money and the value of $C_u$ will be max($\$65 - \$60,0$) = $\$5$. If the stock price goes down, the call option will expire out of the money and the value of $C_d$ will be max($\$45 - \$60,0$) = 0. Using Equation 5.19, we find the hedge ratio to be

$$h_C = \frac{5-0}{65-45} = 0.25,$$

meaning that only 0.25 shares of stock are needed to offset the spread of possible call option payoffs.

Specifically, if we buy 0.25 shares of stock and simultaneously sell the call option, the payoff will be $h_C S_u - C_u = 0.25(65) - 5 = \$11.25$ if the stock price goes up and $h_C S_d - C_d = 0.25(45) - 0 = \$11.25$ if the stock price goes down. Because the payoff of $\$11.25$ is known with certainty, the upfront cost of the strategy must be its present value, $11.25/1.05 = \$10.71$ (rounding to the nearest cent). Because the upfront cost of the shares is $0.25(50) = \$12.50$, the proceeds from the call option we sell must be $12.50 - 10.71 = \$1.79$. We can confirm the $\$1.79$ call price calculation directly by using Equations 5.21 and 5.22. According to Equation 5.22, we have

$$q = \frac{S_0(1+r)^T - S_d}{S_u - S_d} = \frac{50(1+0.05) - 45}{65 - 45} = 0.375,$$

so the price of the call option in Equation 5.21 is

$$C_0 = \frac{(0.375)5 + (1 - 0.375)0}{1.05} = \$1.79.$$

This numerical example illustrates a subtle but important derivatives pricing concept: The forecasted or expected return on the underlying security does not directly affect the arbitrage-free price of the call option. Note that in determining the price of the call option, we never had to specify the actual probabilities that the stock price would go up or down. For example, it might have been a 50/50 chance, so the expected or probability-weighted average ending price of the stock would have been $(0.5)65 + (0.5)45 = \$55$, which is an expected return of $55/50 - 1 = 10\%$. The up/down probabilities could as easily have been 60/40, however, in which case the expected ending stock price would have been $(0.6)65 + (0.4)45 = \$57$ and the expected return would have been $57/50 - 1 = 14\%$. No matter what the up/down probabilities actually are, the arbitrage-free price of the call option remains $1.79.

The algebraic form of Equation 5.21 simply suggests that the up/down probabilities in the underlying stock can be thought of as 0.375 and $1 - 0.375 = 0.625$. If those were the actual probabilities, the expected price of the stock would be $(0.375)65 + (0.625)45 = \$52.50$, for an expected stock return of only $52.50/50 - 1 = 5\%$, the risk-free rate. This algebraic equivalence is the essence of what is called *risk-neutral pricing* in the more formal option-pricing models. It seems counterintuitive that a risky stock should have an expected return that only matches the risk-free rate, but this assumption serves as a shortcut to calculate the arbitrage-free option price.

The simple binomial pricing argument for a put option is similar to the pricing argument for a call, as illustrated in **Figure 5.2**. Again, the security price can move up or down and the payoff of the put option is $P_u$ or $P_d$. The setup analogous to the call option hedge is to buy $h_p$ shares of the stock and simultaneously buy a protective put for a total upfront cost of $h_p S_0 + P_0$. Note that the sign in front of the put price in this setup is positive instead of negative because we are now buying rather than selling the option. The two possible payoffs to this hedge are $h_p S_u + P_u$ and $h_p S_d + P_d$, and the hedge ratio that ensures the two payoffs are equal is

$$h_P = -\frac{P_u - P_d}{S_u - S_d}. \tag{5.23}$$

Note that Equation 5.23 for the put hedge ratio has a negative sign, but the value will actually be nonnegative because $P_u$ is always less than or equal

**Figure 5.2. Simple Binomial Pricing Model for a Put Option**

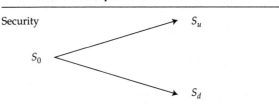

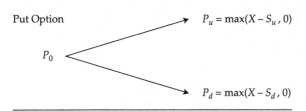

to $P_d$. For example, using the numerical example, we have a stock price of either $S_u$ = \$65 or $S_d$ = \$45. If the stock price goes up, the put with a strike price of \$60 expires out of the money with a value of $P_u$ = max(60 – 65,0) = 0. If the stock price goes down, the put option expires in the money with a value of $P_d$ = max(60 – 45,0) = \$15. Thus, the hedge ratio for the put option is

$$h_P = -\frac{0-15}{65-45} = 0.75,$$

meaning that the hedge is formed by purchasing 0.75 shares of the security for each put option purchased.

As with the call option hedge, the eventual payoff is, by design, certain, so the upfront cost must be the present value of the payoff discounted at the risk-free rate. Again, with several steps of algebra, solving for the current price of the put option gives

$$P_0 = \frac{qP_u + (1-q)P_d}{(1+r)^T}, \tag{5.24}$$

where $q$ is defined as in Equation 5.22. Using Equation 5.24, we find the direct calculation of the put option price to be

$$P_0 = \frac{(0.375)0 + (1-0.375)15}{1.05} = \$8.93.$$

As with the call option price, however, this formulation illustrates that the option price calculation is equivalent to the present value of the risk-neutral probability-weighted average option payoff. But the underlying logic of this arbitrage-free price is that the payoff to the hedge position is

$$h_P S_u + P_u = 0.75(65) + 0 = \$48.75$$

if the stock price goes up and

$$h_P S_d + P_d = 0.75(45) + 15 = \$48.75$$

if the stock price goes down. Because the payoff of $48.75 is known with certainty, the upfront cost of the strategy must be the present value (rounding to the nearest cent) of 48.75/1.05 = $46.43. Because the upfront cost of the shares is 0.75 × 50 = $37.50, then the price of the put option must be 46.43 – 37.50 = $8.93.

We close this section by noting that these call and put option prices are consistent with the European put–call parity condition. Specifically, given the $1.79 price of the call option, the price of the corresponding put option is

$$P_0 = C_0 - S_0 + \frac{X}{(1+r)^T} = 1.79 - 50 + \frac{60}{1.05} = \$8.93,$$

the same as in direct calculation of the put option price found by using Equation 5.24.

## Two-Period Binomial Pricing Model

A slightly more involved extension of the single-period option-pricing framework allows for *two* periods in which the security price can move. In this section, we examine that binomial pricing model for two periods and then, in a subsequent section, extend the hedging logic into multiperiod and "continuous time" models.

**Figure 5.3** illustrates a split in the time to expiration into two equal subperiods, in each of which the stock price may change. If the stock has gone up in the first subperiod, it can then go up again to a price of $S_{uu}$ or down to a price of $S_{ud}$. If the security has gone down in the first subperiod, it can then go up to a price of $S_{du}$ or down to a price of $S_{dd}$. For simplicity, we assume that the up/down path leads to the same price as the down/up path, $S_{ud} = S_{du}$, although the analysis doesn't require this assumption. Similarly, if the security price first goes up, the call option has a value of $C_u$, and if it goes down, the call option is worth $C_d$. In the second subperiod encompassing the option expiration date, the security price can move up or down again, and the value of the option at that point will be defined by its exercise value.

**Figure 5.3.    Two-Period Binomial Pricing Model**

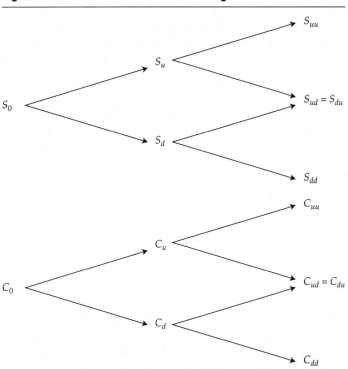

Although this two-period model is more complex than the one-period model, the arbitrage logic is similar. Suppose the security price has gone up, so the security price is at the point $S_u$ in Figure 5.3. With one period left, the value of the call option, $C_u$, can be determined by constructing a riskless hedge on the two possible prices with one period to go, $C_{uu}$ and $C_{ud}$. As we have shown, for the call option, the one-period hedge gives a fully determined price that must hold to avoid arbitrage possibilities.

Now, suppose the security price has gone down in the first period to $S_d$. Again, the value of the call option at this point, $C_d$, can be determined by constructing a riskless hedge on the two possible prices with one period to go, $C_{du}$ and $C_{dd}$. Knowing the two possible option values at the intermediate point, $C_u$ and $C_d$, the arbitrageur can work backwards to determine the current value of the call option, $C_0$.

The key concept is that multiperiod models are solved by working backward from the possible terminal option values. Specifically, the option value at the left side of each branch of the binomial tree is established by using the value of the stock price for that particular path to determine the value of the option at expiration. Hedging logic is then used to establish the intermediate option prices and used again to establish the initial option price.

A common practice in constructing the price path "tree" for the stock (top half of Figure 5.3) is to assume the same proportions in price movement over time. For example, if the stock price goes up by 10% or down by 5% in the first period, then the price is again assumed to go up by 10% or down by 5% in the second period. As long as this convention is followed, the value of the risk-neutral probability variable, $q$, remains constant over time and across different price paths. In that case, formulas for the intermediate-date call option values can be substituted into the formula for the current call value, giving a compact solution of

$$C_0 = \frac{qC_u + (1-q)C_d}{(1+r)^{T/2}}$$

$$= \frac{q^2 C_{uu} + 2q(1-q)C_{ud} + (1-q)^2 C_{dd}}{(1+r)^T}. \tag{5.25}$$

Notice that the intermediate-term call option values in Equation 5.25 are discounted for only half the total time to option expiration, $T/2$. However, the intermediate-term option values, $C_u$ and $C_d$, are, in turn, based on discounting the final call value for the remaining time to option expiration, $T/2$, so full-period discounting shows up in the denominator of the last term. Also, be aware that although the risk-neutral probability variable, $q$, remains constant over time, the hedge ratio, $h$, does not. For example, if the stock price goes up in the first period, arbitrageurs will generally need to increase the hedge ratio because the call option will become more sensitive to subsequent stock price changes. (In Black–Scholes option-pricing terminology, this condition is known as a *higher delta*.) If the stock price goes down in the first period, arbitrageurs may need to decrease the hedge ratio. The process of changing the amount of the underlying security owned over time to maintain a riskless position is known as *dynamic hedging*, and it is a common practice by those who are trying to exploit arbitrage opportunities in the option markets.

For a numerical example of the two-period binomial process, suppose, again, that the stock price initially starts at $50 but can take on three possible prices at the expiration of the option. Specifically, for each of the two subperiods, the price can increase by 20% or decrease by 10%. If the price goes up 20% to $60 in the first subperiod, then it might go up by another 20% to $72 in the second period or go down by 10% to $54. If the stock price goes down 10% in the first subperiod to $45, then it might subsequently go up 20% to $54 or down by 10% to $40.50. For these prices, the final payoffs to a call option with a strike price of $60 are

$$C_{uu} = \max(S_{uu} - X, 0) = \max(72 - 60, 0) = 12;$$
$$C_{ud} = \max(S_{ud} - X, 0) = \max(54 - 60, 0) = 0;$$
$$C_{dd} = \max(S_{dd} - X, 0) = \max(40.50 - 60, 0) = 0.$$

Thus, the call option expires in the money for only one of the three possible expiration-date values of the stock.

Suppose, as before, that the total time to option expiration is one year, so each of the two subperiods is six months. For numerical simplicity, we will set the six-month risk-free interest rate at 2%, so the effective annual rate is $(1.0 + 0.02)^2 - 1 = 4.04\%$. With these parameter values, the risk-neutral probability of an up move in the security price is

$$q = \frac{1.02 - 0.9}{1.2 - 0.9}$$
$$= 0.4$$

for each subperiod. The arbitrage-free price of the call option if the stock goes up in the first subperiod is

$$C_u = \frac{(0.4)\,12 + (1 - 0.4)\,0}{1 + 0.02}$$
$$= \$4.71,$$

and the call price if the stock goes down in the first subperiod is

$$C_d = \frac{(0.4)\,0 + (1 - 0.4)\,0}{1 + 0.02}$$
$$= \$0.$$

Note that the dynamic hedge ratio if the stock goes up in the first period will be $(12 - 0)/(72 - 54) = 0.667$ (i.e., two-thirds) whereas the dynamic hedge ratio if the stock goes down will be $(0 - 0)/(54 - 40.50) = 0.00$. If the stock goes down in the first period, no hedge is needed because the call option value does not vary between the two subsequently possible stock prices. By working backward, we can now determine the current arbitrage-free price of the call option as

$$C_0 = \frac{(0.40)4.71 + (1 - 0.40)0}{1 + 0.02}$$
$$= \$1.85,$$

which can also be verified by a more direct hedging calculation using the initial call option hedge ratio of $(4.71 - 0)/(60 - 45) = 0.314$.

The final payoffs to a put option with a strike price of $60 are

$$P_{uu} = \max(X - S_{uu}, 0) = \max(60 - 72, 0) = 0;$$
$$P_{ud} = \max(X - S_{ud}, 0) = \max(60 - 54, 0) = 6;$$
$$P_{dd} = \max(X - S_{dd}, 0) = \max(60 - 40.50, 0) = 19.50.$$

In other words, the put option expires out of the money for the highest possible stock price but in the money for the other two values of the stock. The arbitrage-free price of the put option if the stock goes up in the first subperiod is

$$P_u = \frac{(0.40)\,0 + (1-0.40)\,6}{1+0.02} = \$3.53,$$

and the put price if the stock goes down in the first subperiod is

$$P_d = \frac{(0.40)\,6 + (1-0.40)\,19.50}{1+0.02} = \$13.82.$$

Using the single compact version of the formula in Equation 5.25, we find the current value of the put option to be

$$P_0 = \frac{qP_u + (1-q)P_d}{(1+r)^{T/2}} = \frac{(0.40)3.53 + (0.60)13.82}{1+0.02} = \$9.52.$$

The same put price is derived from the expanded version of Equation 5.25,

$$P_0 = \frac{q^2 P_{uu} + 2q(1-q)P_{ud} + (1-q)^2 P_{dd}}{(1+r)^T}$$

$$= \frac{(0.40)^2\,0 + 2(0.40)(0.60)6 + (0.60)^2\,19.50}{(1+0.02)^2} = \$9.52.$$

The dynamic hedge ratio for the put option if the stock goes up in the first period will be $(6-0)/(72-54) = 0.33$ (one-third), whereas the put hedge ratio will be $(19.50-6)/(54-40.50) = 1.00$ if the stock price goes down. The hedge ratio of 1.0 is needed because after the initial decline in the stock price, the spread of subsequent possible put option values equals the spread of possible stock prices. As the reader will observe in the more sophisticated Black–Scholes formula, the European put option hedge ratio is always 1.0 minus the European call option hedge ratio. For example, the initial hedge ratio for the put option is $(13.82-3.52)/(60-45) = 0.686$, or 1.0 minus the previously calculated call option hedge of 0.314.

Because they are European options, the call and put prices we just calculated are consistent with put–call parity. Specifically, the put price can be calculated directly from the call price by

$$P_0 = C_0 - S_0 + \frac{X}{(1+r)^T} = 1.85 - 50 + \frac{60}{(1+0.02)^2} = \$9.52.$$

The price of the put option would be somewhat higher if early exercise were allowed. As we calculated, the riskless hedge value for the put option

©2013 The Research Foundation of CFA Institute

if the stock price goes down to \$45 in the first subperiod is \$13.82, but this amount is below the exercise value at that point of $60 - 45 = \$15.00$. If the options are American, then arbitrageurs will anticipate the possibility of early exercise, so the initial price of the put option will be based on the intermediate-term put values of \$3.53 and \$15.00, not \$3.53 and \$13.82. Thus, the initial price of an American put option from the compact version of Equation 5.25 will be

$$P_0 = \frac{qP_u + (1-q)P_d}{(1+r)^{T/2}} = \frac{(0.40)3.53 + (0.60)15.00}{1+0.02} = \$10.21,$$

which is 69 cents higher than the European put price of \$9.52.

The corresponding American call option price would *not* be higher in this case because we have assumed that the underlying stock does not pay a dividend, so early exercise of the call option would never be desirable.

## Multiperiod Binomial and Black–Scholes Models

The process of dividing the time until option expiration into smaller and smaller portions can be continued for three, four, and in general, $N$ subperiods. Although more complex branching processing can be modeled, a common practice is to assume that branches recombine, as in the assumption that $S_{ud} = S_{du}$ in the two-period tree of Figure 5.3. In that case, the number of terminal stock prices will be the number of subperiods plus 1.

For example, **Figure 5.4** shows the price tree for a three-period model and four terminal stock prices. To arrive at increasingly more accurate arbitrage-free prices for the option at time zero, the arbitrageur must take care to ensure that the jump sizes and present value discounting in the branching process are consistent with the increasingly shorter subperiods. For a time-to-expiration

**Figure 5.4.     Multiperiod Binomial Model**

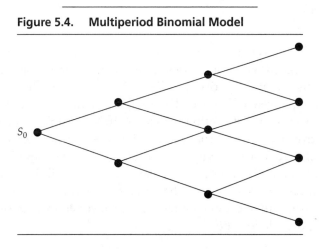

volatility parameter σ and price trend μ, the initial up and down jumps can be calculated by

$$S_u = S_0\, e^{\mu/T + \sigma\sqrt{T/N}}$$

and                                                                                           (5.26)

$$S_d = S_0\, e^{\mu/T - \sigma\sqrt{T/N}},$$

where $e^{()}$ indicates exponentiation ($e$ being the natural number 2.17828).

The numerical choice for the price trend parameter, μ, can be based on an expected return for the stock or, as is more common, the risk-free rate, consistent with the notion of risk-neutral pricing. In the limit, as $N$ increases to a large number, this parameter choice will not affect the final calculation of the current option price.

As the number of subperiods increases, more and more terms are added to the compact formulas for the current option prices discussed in the prior section. The probabilities of each possible outcome combine according to the binomial distribution—for example, $q^3$ for the possibility of three consecutive moves up or $q^2(1-q)$ for two moves up and then one move down. In the limit, the binomial process converges to the well-known Black–Scholes model for a European option with no cash distributions:

$$C_0 = S_0\, N(d_1) - X\, e^{-rT} N(d_2),\tag{5.27}$$

where

$$d_1 = \frac{\ln(S_0/X) + (r + \sigma^2/2)T}{\sigma\sqrt{T}}$$

and                                                                                           (5.28)

$$d_2 = \frac{\ln(S_0/X) + (r - \sigma^2/2)T}{\sigma\sqrt{T}}.$$

The Black–Scholes model in Equations 5.27 and 5.28 uses a number of functions associated with continuous-time financial mathematics. The function ln( ) is the natural logarithm, called LN( ) in Excel. The function $e^{()}$ is exponentiation, called EXP( ) in Excel. The function $N($ ) is the cumulative standard normal distribution, called NORM.S.DIST( ) in Excel with the cumulative flag set to "true." In continuous-time mathematics, present values are calculated by the term $e^{-rT}$ instead of the more familiar $1/(1 + R)^T$ formulation used in discrete time. The parameter $T$ is still the time to option expiration, measured in years, but the risk-free rate, $r$, is a continuously compounded return. Discrete annual rates can be converted to a continuous-time rate by using the relationship

$$r = \ln(1+R). \tag{5.29}$$

For example, if the discrete annual risk-free rate is 5.00%, then the continuously compounded rate is $\ln(1 + 0.05) = 4.879\%$. For example, a present value of $X = 100$ discounted for three months (0.25 years) can be calculated either in discrete time as $100/(1 + 0.05)^{0.25} = \$98.79$ or in continuous time as $100 \times e^{-0.04879(0.25)} = \$98.79$.

With its assumption of continuous time, the Black–Scholes model has some recognizable similarities to the multiperiod binomial model. Both involve probabilities, and both include a present value calculation at the risk-free rate over the time to expiration of the option. The inputs to the Black–Scholes model include the current stock price, $S_0$; the option exercise price, $X$; the time to option expiration, $T$; and the continuously compounded risk-free rate, $r$. The only new parameter is a measure of annualized volatility in the underlying security price, $\sigma$, which conceptually replaces the spread of possible stock prices in the binomial model.

The Black–Scholes price for a European put option can be derived from the European call price and the put–call parity relationship with continuous compounding:

$$\begin{aligned} p_0 &= c_0 - S_0 + Xe^{-rT} \\ &= -S_0\left[1 - N(d_1)\right] + Xe^{-rT}\left[1 - N(d_2)\right], \end{aligned} \tag{5.30}$$

where $d_1$ and $d_2$ are defined as in Equations 5.28.

We can illustrate Black–Scholes model calculations with some simple parameters. Suppose the underlying stock price is $S_0 = \$100$ and we are pricing at-the-money European-style options with a strike price of $X = \$100$. The options have one month to expiration, so $T = 1/12$ (approximately 0.8333), and the continuously compounded annual risk-free rate is 2%. We will use an underlying security volatility estimate of 40%. Using Equations 5.28 and the standard cumulative normal distribution function, we have

$$\begin{aligned} N(d_1) &= N\left[\frac{\ln(100/100) + (0.02 + 0.40^2/2)(0.0833)}{0.40\sqrt{0.0833}}\right] \\ &= N(0.07217) \\ &= 0.529 \end{aligned}$$

and

$$\begin{aligned} N(d_2) &= N\left[\frac{\ln(100/100) + (0.02 - 0.40^2/2)(0.0833)}{0.40\sqrt{0.0833}}\right] \\ &= N(-0.04330) \\ &= 0.483. \end{aligned}$$

Inserting these values in Equation 5.27 gives us the current price of the call option as

$$C_0 = 100(0.529) - 100\, e^{-0.02(0.0833)}(0.483)$$
$$= \$4.68.$$

Using Equation 5.30, we find the corresponding put option to be

$$P_0 = -100\,(1-0.529) + 100\, e^{-0.02(0.0833)}(1-0.483)$$
$$= \$4.52.$$

With the Black–Scholes formulas, we can easily see how the call and put prices respond to changes in the various input parameters. The two curves in **Figure 5.5** plot the call and put prices for changes in the underlying stock price from \$80 to \$100, with the other parameters held constant. As the security price increases, the call price increases from almost zero to about \$20 but the put price decreases from about \$20 to almost zero. The prices of the two options are equal when the stock hits the present value of the strike price, just below \$100.

**Figure 5.5.    Relationship of Option Prices to the Security Price**

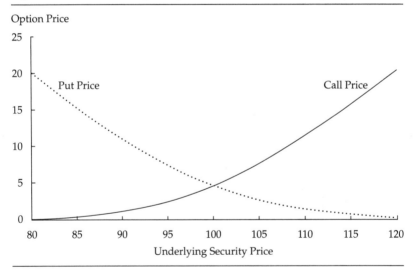

**Figure 5.6** plots how the option prices change with time to expiration with the stock price held at \$100. For these two at-the-money options, the entire option price is time value. For at-the-money options, call options have a slightly higher price than put options because of the positive riskless interest rate. But as the options near expiration, the time value decays toward zero.

**Figure 5.7** shows how the option prices change for different volatility parameters. As previously mentioned, the at-the-money call price is slightly higher than

**Figure 5.6. Relationship of Option Prices to Time to Expiration**

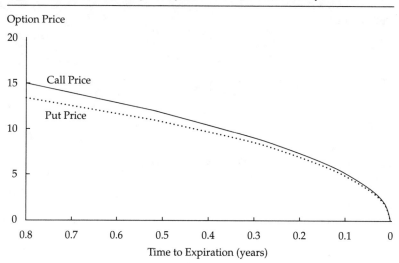

**Figure 5.7. Relationship of Option Prices to Volatility**

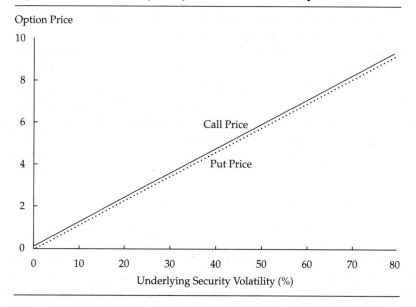

the put price, but both option prices increase in value almost linearly with volatility. Option prices increase with volatility because the range of possible stock prices at expiration grows; thus, the potential payoffs to each option grow.

**Figure 5.8** shows how the call and put option prices respond to changes in the risk-free interest rate. The price of the call option increases with an increase in interest rates, and the price of the put option decreases. These

**Figure 5.8.    Relationship of Option Prices to Interest Rates**

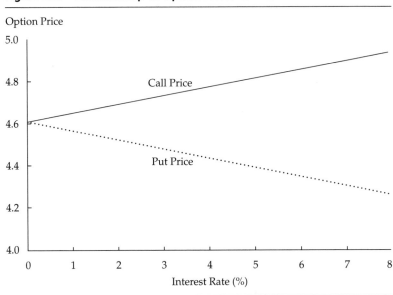

effects are consistent with the opportunity cost of early exercise implied in the time value of the put and call option prices discussed earlier.

Of all the inputs to the Black–Scholes option price, the volatility estimate is the most subjective. The price of the underlying stock is quoted by the market daily (in fact, continuously), and the strike price and option expiration dates are specified up front and do not change. Risk-free borrowing and lending rates for arbitrageurs are generally close to LIBOR or some other market-based short-term interest rate. Analysts can use historical returns to calculate what the volatility has been in the past, although these calculations need to be adjusted for the frequency of returns to arrive at an annualized number. If daily returns are used, the variance (standard deviation squared) is typically multiplied by 250, the number of trading days per year. If monthly returns are used, the variance is multiplied by 12.

Alternatively, an analyst can use all the other inputs to the model to infer a volatility estimate from the observed market prices for the option. This estimate of volatility is called the option's *implied volatility*. The volatility implied by the current option price can then be compared with historical volatility. Implied volatility higher than historical volatility may indicate that the option is expensive relative to historical measures; lower implied volatility may indicate that the option is cheap. **Table 5.1** gives the volatility implied by various call option prices, with the other previously discussed input parameters, and using the Solver functionality within Excel. The volatility estimate of 40% used throughout this section results in a call option price of $4.68, so the implied volatilities for the $4.00 and $5.00 quotes are, respectively, lower and higher than this estimate.

Table 5.1. Implied Volatilities from
the Black–Scholes Model

| Call Price Quote | Implied Volatility |
|---|---|
| $1.00 | 7.95% |
| 2.00 | 16.65 |
| 3.00 | 25.35 |
| 4.00 | 35.04 |
| 5.00 | 42.75 |
| 6.00 | 51.46 |
| 7.00 | 60.18 |
| 8.00 | 68.91 |
| 9.00 | 77.65 |

A simple analytic approximation of the implied volatility can be calculated for the average price of a put–call pair that is close to the money. Specifically, Brenner and Subrahmanyam (1988) show that the implied volatility resulting from a Black–Scholes model can be approximated by

$$\sigma = \frac{C_0 + P_0}{2S_0} \sqrt{\frac{2\pi}{T}}. \qquad (5.31)$$

For example, the at-the-money $100-strike-price options with exactly one month (1/12 year) to expiration were calculated previously as $C_0 = \$4.68$ and $P_0 = \$4.52$. Putting these values into the analytic approximation, Equation 5.31, give

$$\sigma = \frac{4.68 + 4.52}{2(100)} \sqrt{\frac{2\pi}{1/12}}$$
$$= 39.94\%,$$

which is quite close to the actual volatility of 40.00% used by the Black–Scholes formula to calculate the option prices earlier in this section. The put and call options used for the approximation need to have the same strike price and maturity, and the best approximation of implied volatility is based on put–call pairs that are close to being at the money.

## Black–Scholes Option Price Assumptions

Like any formula, the Black–Scholes model depends on a number of simplifying assumptions. First and foremost, the Black–Scholes formula is a continuous-time extension of the binomial model with no early exercise. Thus, the basic formula strictly applies only to European-style options. Also, the formula is based on the assumption that the underlying security return is lognormally distributed and that the volatility of the underlying security is constant over time. In essence, the model does not allow for instantaneous jumps in the security price. Over a very short period of time, the security can move a little but not a large amount. The original model also assumes no dividends or cash payments on the underlying security and assumes constant interest rates.

Researchers have tried to develop models to relax most of these assumptions, and many of today's models are variations of the original 1972 Black–Scholes formula. Interestingly, the mathematically more sophisticated Black–Scholes formula was developed before simple binomial pricing methods were developed. Only later did researchers show that the binomial model converges to the Black–Scholes model under consistently applied up and down price movements in the underlying security (see Sharpe 1985; Cox, Ross, and Rubinstein 1979).

The easiest assumption to relax in the basic Black–Scholes model is the requirement of no cash distributions in the underlying security. For known discrete dividends, the current stock price needs to be adjusted by the present value of the dividends before being used in the Black–Scholes model. For example, suppose the current stock price is $S_0$ with a cash dividend, $D$, paid at time $t$ prior to the option expiration at time $T$. Using continuous-time mathematics, the dividend-adjusted stock price is

$$S_0^* = S_0 - De^{-rt}, \tag{5.32}$$

and it can be substituted for the input parameter $S_0$ wherever it occurs in the basic Black–Scholes formula in Equations 5.27 and 5.28. The incorporation of the dividend payment slightly reduces the price of a call option and increases the price of a put option, similar to the effect of a small decrease in the actual stock price.

Another approach to adjusting the stock price is to assume that the dividend is paid continuously at a known yield (see Merton 1973a). This assumption is useful because it can approximate the impact of dividends on an equity index option because the many different stocks in an index pay dividends at different times. The adjustment is as follows: If $d$ represents the aggregate annual dividend yield, the adjusted stock price for an index option with expiration date $T$ is

$$S_0^* = S_0 e^{-dT}. \tag{5.33}$$

Options on foreign exchange rates can also be put into this framework. In the case of these options, the riskless asset denominated in the foreign currency pays continuous interest at rate $r_f$, similar to a continuous dividend yield. That is, if $S_0$ represents the underlying exchange rate (rather than, say, the price of a stock), the modification involves substituting

$$S_0^* = S_0 e^{-r_f T} \tag{5.34}$$

for each occurrence of $S_0$ in the standard Black–Scholes formula in Equations 5.27 and 5.28.

The dividend and foreign exchange adjustments presented here assume that the options cannot be exercised early, but more complicated variations of the Black–Scholes model for American-style options do allow for early exercise. Generally, American-style options are priced by the use of multiperiod binomial pricing techniques, which can be programmed to model complex early-exercise possibilities.

The following summarizes the variations on the Black–Scholes formulas we have discussed so far:

| | | |
|---|---|---|
| Discrete cash payout: | $S_0^* = S_0 - De^{-rt}$ | where $D$ = payout at time $t$ |
| Continuous cash payout: | $S_0^* = S_0 e^{-dT}$ | where $d$ is the annual continuous rate |
| Currency option: | $S_0^* = S_0 e^{-r_f T}$ | where $r_f$ is the annual foreign interest rate |

Relaxing some of the other assumptions of the Black–Scholes model is more difficult than modifying it for cash distributions. Some attempts have been made to develop models in which the underlying security price is not lognormally distributed. For example, Bookstaber and McDonald (1985) developed models with more general probability distributions, of which the lognormal distribution is a special case. Relaxing the assumptions of constant variance and interest rates is even more difficult. Specialized models for fixed-income options have been developed, however, by relaxing the assumption of constant interest rates (see Dattatreya and Fabozzi 1989; Black, Derman, and Toy 1990).

## Options on Futures

An option on a futures contract differs from a direct option on the underlying security in that the buyer of the futures option establishes a position in a futures contract upon exercise instead of in the underlying security. In many respects, an investor can think of the futures as simply another underlying security to which the option is tied. As with regular options, buyers of futures options must pay a price for the option, sellers receive the option price, and sellers are generally required to post margin. After exercise of the option, both the long and short futures positions are required to post margin and mark to market, as with any other investor in futures. Many futures options expire on the same date as the futures contract itself, although the U.S. Treasury bond and note futures options are an exception. Specifically, options on T-bond and T-note futures expire a month before the futures contract, so the investor can take full advantage of the delivery window for T-bond and T-note futures contracts.

The put–call parity relationship for European futures options is similar to that for cash options. A riskless payoff at time $T$ can be constructed by buying futures, selling a futures call option, and buying a futures put option. The contingency table follows.

|  | $F_T < X$ | $F_T > X$ |
|---|---|---|
| Purchase futures | $F_T - F_0$ | $F_T - F_0$ |
| Sell call | 0 | $-(F_T - X)$ |
| Purchase put | $X - F_T$ | 0 |
| Total payoff | $X - F_0$ | $X - F_0$ |

Because the payoff from this strategy is riskless, the present value of this payoff must equal the net amount of funds invested,

$$p_0 - c_0 = \frac{X - F_0}{(1+r)^T}, \tag{5.35}$$

which is somewhat similar to the put–call parity relationship for cash options. Indeed, if the futures contract is priced like a forward contract, $F_0 = S_0(1 + r)^T$, the price of a European call is

$$c_0 = p_0 + S_0 - \frac{X}{(1+r)^T}, \tag{5.36}$$

which is simply the cash put–call parity relationship. If the option on a futures contract cannot be exercised early and the option and futures expire at the same time, the European futures option is no different from a European cash option. This characteristic results from the fact that, at expiration, the futures price and cash price will be equal. The fact that the futures price and security price are different before expiration does not matter if the futures option cannot be exercised early.

Fischer Black (1976) developed a variation of the Black–Scholes model to apply to a European futures option:

$$c_0 = F_0 e^{-rT} N(d_1) - X e^{-rT} N(d_2), \tag{5.37}$$

where $F_0$ is the current futures price and

$$d_1 = \frac{\ln(F_0 / X) + \sigma^2 T / 2}{\sigma\sqrt{T}}$$

and $\tag{5.38}$

$$d_2 = \frac{\ln(F_0 / X) - \sigma^2 T / 2}{\sigma\sqrt{T}}.$$

Notice that the Black model for futures options in Equation 5.37 is similar to the more common Black–Scholes model in Equation 5.27, with $F_0$ replacing $S_0$, and

**94**

the formulas for $d_1$ and $d_2$ in Equation 5.38 have one fewer term than in Equation 5.27. Indeed, the Black model simply substitutes the present value of the futures price (using continuous compounding) for the cash price by using the formula

$$S_0^* = F_0 e^{-rT}. \tag{5.39}$$

For European options, the value for a futures put option can be derived from the put–call parity relationship (using continuous compounding) together with the Black model for the value of the futures call option:

$$p_0 = c_0 + (X - F_0)e^{-rT}. \tag{5.40}$$

Substitution of the value for the futures call option gives the futures put option price as

$$p_0 = -F_0 e^{-rT}\left[1 - N(d_1)\right] + Xe^{-rT}\left[1 - N(d_2)\right]. \tag{5.41}$$

One of the major differences between futures options and regular cash options occurs when the options are American and can thus be exercised early. Although exercising an American call option early is not advisable unless there is a large cash distribution on the underlying security, exercising the American call option on a futures contract may be desirable if the payoff from early exercise is greater than the value of the corresponding option without early exercise:

$$F_0 - X > c_0. \tag{5.42}$$

Substituting for the value of the call option using put–call parity for European futures options gives the equivalent condition as

$$p_0 < (F_0 - X)(1 - e^{-rT}), \tag{5.43}$$

which can occur if the call option is far enough in the money to result in a small put price.

Exercising a futures put option early is desirable if the payoff from early exercise is greater than the value of the option:

$$X - F_0 > p_0. \tag{5.44}$$

Substituting for the value of the put option using put–call parity for European futures options gives the equivalent condition as

$$c_0 < (X - F_0)(1 - e^{-rT}), \tag{5.45}$$

which can occur if the put option is far enough in the money to result in a small call price. The logic is that if the put or call options are deep enough in the money, their time value components are small and the option value is dominated by intrinsic value. The interest available to be earned on the intrinsic value makes early exercise of the futures options worthwhile because the investor will lose the time value of the option but gain an even greater value from being able to invest in the intrinsic value.

# 6. Option Contracts: Hedging Relationships

In this chapter, we describe some of the techniques used to monitor option positions and manage option-related exposures. The first section deals with how an option price moves as its parameters change, and the second section addresses how to use these measures to help control the risk in a portfolio. In the final section, we explore some alternative ways to create option-like effects in a portfolio.

## Sensitivity Measures

Option analysts use a series of Greek letters to describe how a call option's price changes as its parameters change, as shown in **Table 6.1**. The first and most important "greek" is *delta*, $\Delta$, which describes the change in the option price resulting from a change in the price of the underlying security. The delta of an option is also known as the *hedge ratio* because it specifies the number of shares in the underlying security needed to offset a change in option value resulting from changes in the underlying security's price. Mathematically, delta is the partial derivative of the option price with respect to a change in $S_0$, the underlying security price. Another greek, *gamma*, $\gamma$, describes the change in option price for a change in delta—in other words, the *second* partial derivative of the option price with respect to a change in the security price.

### Table 6.1   Call Option Sensitivity Measures

| Name | Sensitivity to | Notation |
|------|----------------|----------|
| Delta | Security price | $\Delta_c = \dfrac{\partial C_0}{\partial S_0}$ |
| Gamma | Delta | $\gamma_c = \dfrac{\partial^2 C_0}{\partial S_0^2}$ |
| Theta | Time to expiration | $\theta_c = -\dfrac{\partial C_0}{\partial T}$ |
| Rho | Interest rate | $\rho_c = \dfrac{\partial C_0}{\partial r}$ |
| Vega | Volatility | $\nu_c = \dfrac{\partial C_0}{\partial \sigma}$ |

A third greek is *theta*, θ, the change in option price because of the passage of time. The definition of theta includes a negative sign because option prices, both calls and puts, decrease as they get closer to expiration. In other words, as the option nears expiration, the time value component approaches zero, so the option price is either the exercise value (if the option expires in the money) or zero (if the option expires out of the money). A fourth greek is *rho*, ρ, which measures the sensitivity of the option price to a change in interest rates. The final measure of option price sensitivity is *vega*, which is not actually a letter in the Greek alphabet, so the notation ν (Greek letter *nu*) is used. Vega measures the sensitivity of the option price to changes in the volatility of the underlying security. **Table 6.2** gives the formulas for each of the five sensitivity measures in terms of the Black–Scholes valuation model. Notice that the formulas for gamma and vega are the same for both put and call options.

**Table 6.2  Option Sensitivity Formulas in Terms of the Black–Scholes Model**

| Name (measure) | Call Option | Put Option |
|---|---|---|
| Delta (security price) | $\Delta_c = N(d_1)$ | $\Delta_p = \Delta_c - 1$ |
| Gamma (delta) | $\gamma_c = \dfrac{n(d_1)}{S_0 \sigma \sqrt{T}}$ | $\gamma_p = \gamma_c$ |
| Theta (time to expiration) | $\theta_c = -\dfrac{S_0 \sigma n(d_1)}{2\sqrt{T}} - rXe^{-rT}N(d_2)$ | $\theta_p = \theta_c + rXe^{-rT}$ |
| Rho (interest rate) | $\rho_c = XTe^{-rT}N(d_2)$ | $\rho_p = \rho_c - XTe^{-rT}$ |
| Vega (volatility) | $\nu_c = S_0\sqrt{T}n(d_1)$ | $\nu_p = \nu_c$ |

*Note:* The term $n(d)$ is the standard normal probability density function, $n(d) = e^{-d^2/2}/\sqrt{2\pi}$, and $N(d)$ is the standard normal cumulative distribution function, $N(d) = \int_{-\infty}^{d} n(d)$. Strictly speaking, these formulas apply to European options, not to American options, which allow for early exercise.

**Table 6.3** provides example values for each of the sensitivity measures. The numerical examples in Table 6.3 are for options with an exercise price of $100 that are currently at the money (i.e., the underlying security price is at $100) with one month to expiration, where the annual continuously compounded interest rate is 2% and the underlying security volatility is

**Table 6.3   Example Values for Call and Put Option Sensitivity Measures**

| Name | Call | Put |
|------|------|-----|
| Delta (per 1.00) | 0.529 | −0.471 |
| Gamma (per delta) | 0.034 | 0.034 |
| Theta (per day) | −0.073 | −0.067 |
| Rho (per 1%) | 0.040 | −0.043 |
| Vega (per 1%) | 0.115 | 0.115 |

*Note:* The assumptions are $S_0 = \$100$, $X = \$100$, $T = 1/12$ (30.4 days), $r = 2.00\%$, and $\sigma = 40.0\%$.

40%. For example, the call option delta is 0.529, meaning that if the underlying security price rises by $1.00, the price of the call option will increase by 52.9 cents.

**Delta.** The delta on a put option is closely related to the delta on a call option, as shown by the put–call parity relationship in Equation 5.30. Taking the derivative of both sides of Equation 5.30 with respect to $S_0$ gives

$$\Delta_P = \Delta_C - 1, \tag{6.1}$$

as shown at the top of the last column in Table 6.2. Note that the delta of a put option is always equal to the delta of the corresponding call option minus 1.

Deltas on call options range from 0, for deeply out-of-the-money options, to 1, for deeply in-the-money options. Thus, the delta of the corresponding put option will be a negative value between −1 and 0.

Option deltas can be used to calculate beta (sensitivity to the market) in equity markets and duration (sensitivity to interest rates) in fixed-income markets. In equity markets, beta is a common measure of the sensitivity of an individual stock price to changes in the general market (i.e., to changes in a market index or benchmark). Specifically, beta measures the *percentage* change in stock price for any percentage change in a market index. The market beta of a call option is equal to the beta of the stock multiplied by the ratio of the prices of the stock and call option, $S_0/C_0$, multiplied by the delta of the call option:

$$\beta_c = \beta_S \left( \frac{S_0}{C_0} \right) \Delta_c. \tag{6.2}$$

Similarly, modified duration in fixed-income markets measures the percentage change in the bond price for a change in yield. The modified duration of a call option is equal to the modified duration of the underlying bond, $D_B^*$, multiplied by the ratio of the bond and call option prices, $B_0/C_0$, multiplied by the call option delta:

$$D_c^* = D_B^* \left( \frac{B_0}{C_0} \right) \Delta_C. \tag{6.3}$$

The equity market beta and fixed-income duration for put options have the same form and can be found by substituting the delta and price of the put option for the delta and price of the call option in Equations 6.2 and 6.3.

**Figure 6.1** plots the Black–Scholes model call and put option deltas for underlying security prices from \$80 to \$120 for the sample numerical values in Table 6.3. As shown in Figure 6.1, when the call option is deeply out of the money, the delta is close to 0, and when the call option is deeply in the money, the delta approaches 1. The delta of the call option is always positive, meaning that the option price always *increases* with increases in the underlying security price. The delta of the put option is always negative, meaning that the option price always *decreases* with increases in the underlying security price. Note the constant gap between the delta of the call and the delta of the put, which occurs because the delta of the put option is equal to the delta of the call option minus 1.

**Figure 6.1. Relationship of Delta to Underlying Security Price**

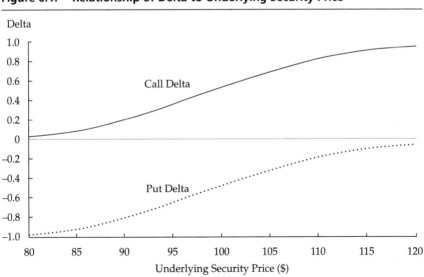

Delta is also sensitive to the time to expiration of the option. **Figure 6.2** shows how the delta plots change for a longer-maturity option—that is, three months to expiration instead of only one month. The delta curve tends to flatten out with a longer-maturity option. In other words, the sensitivity of the option price to changes in the underlying security price is more stable for a longer-maturity option.

**Figure 6.2.  Relationship of Delta to Underlying Security Price for Three Months vs. One Month to Expiration**

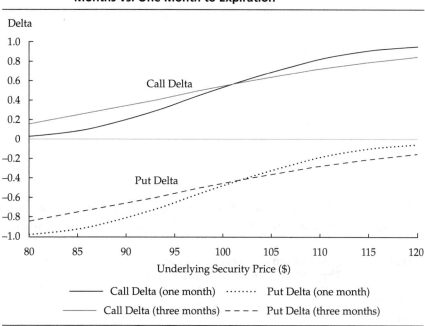

**Gamma.** Because delta is probably the most important sensitivity measure of all the greeks, analysts also measure *changes* in delta in response to changes in the underlying security price. So, gamma is a second derivative with respect to security price, somewhat like the use of convexity in addition to duration by fixed-income analysts.

**Figure 6.3** plots the gamma of the put–call pair (both have the same gamma) used in the previous figures for various levels of the underlying security price. Gamma is highest (change of delta is greatest) when options are near the money. When options are way out of the money or way in the money, the delta plot in Figure 6.1 is not as steep, so gamma is smaller. At its peak, the gamma plot in Figure 6.3 indicates that a $1 move in the underlying security price will increase the delta by about 0.035. For example, if the call option delta happened to be 0.500, a $1 increase in the security price would increase the delta to 0.535.

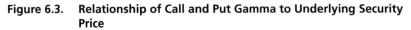

**Figure 6.3. Relationship of Call and Put Gamma to Underlying Security Price**

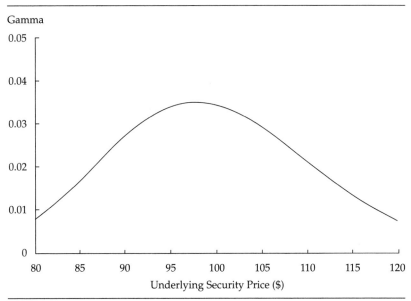

Like delta, gamma is also sensitive to the time to expiration of the option. **Figure 6.4** shows that the gamma curve flattens out for longer-maturity

**Figure 6.4. Relationship of Gamma to Underlying Security Price for Three Months vs. One Month to Expiration**

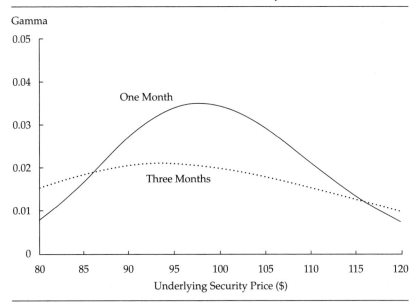

options, meaning that the change in delta is less variable for any change in security price for longer-maturity options.

**Theta.** **Figure 6.5** plots the sensitivity of option prices to time to expiration, where theta is measured as price change per day instead of year. Theta is, by definition, negative for both the call and the put options, indicating that options are "wasting" assets in that, with the other parameters held constant, their values go down over time. Note in Figure 6.5 that the call option is slightly more sensitive to time decay than is the put option for any given security price. For example, at its extreme point, when the options are near the money, the call option will lose a little more than $0.07 a day in value whereas the put option will lose a little less than $0.07 a day.

**Figure 6.5.    Relationship of (Daily) Theta to Underlying Security Price**

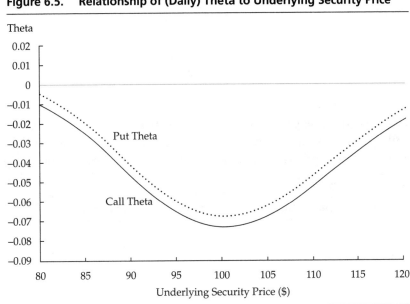

Time decay is also sensitive to the expiration date of the option, as shown in **Figure 6.6** for the call option. Specifically, time decay is more constant across the range of moneyness with an option that is further away from expiration.

**Rho.** **Figure 6.7** plots rho, which measures the sensitivity of the call and put option prices to changes in interest rates. The rho for call options is always positive; that is, the call option price increases for increases in the interest rate. The rho for put options is always negative. The right to buy later at some fixed price is worth more when interest rates are higher, and the right to sell later at a fixed price is worth less. When the call option is deeply out of the

**Figure 6.6.  Relationship of (Daily) Theta to Underlying Security Price for Three Months vs. One Month to Expiration**

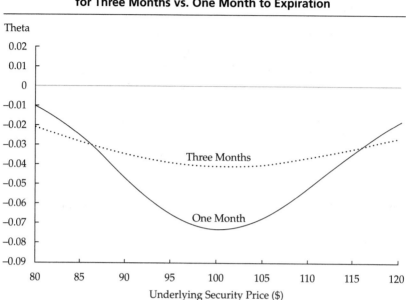

money, it has little sensitivity to interest rates, but sensitivity increases when the call option is in the money. The numerical value of rho indicates that for at-the-money call options with an underlying security price of $100, a 1 percentage point increase in the interest rate would increase the call option price

**Figure 6.7.  Relationship of Rho to Underlying Security Price**

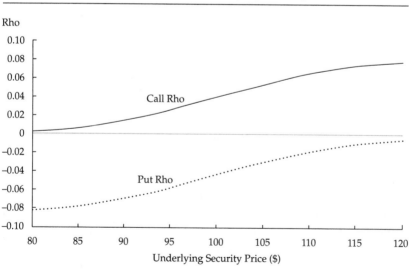

by about 4 cents. The put option is also more sensitive to interest rate changes when it is in the money than when it is out of the money, but as stated, the rho for a put option is negative.

Interest rate sensitivity is also a function of the time to expiration, as shown in **Figure 6.8** for the call option. Intuitively, the values of longer-term options are more sensitive to interest rate changes than are near-term options.

**Figure 6.8. Relationship of Rho to Underlying Security Price for Three Months vs. One Month to Expiration**

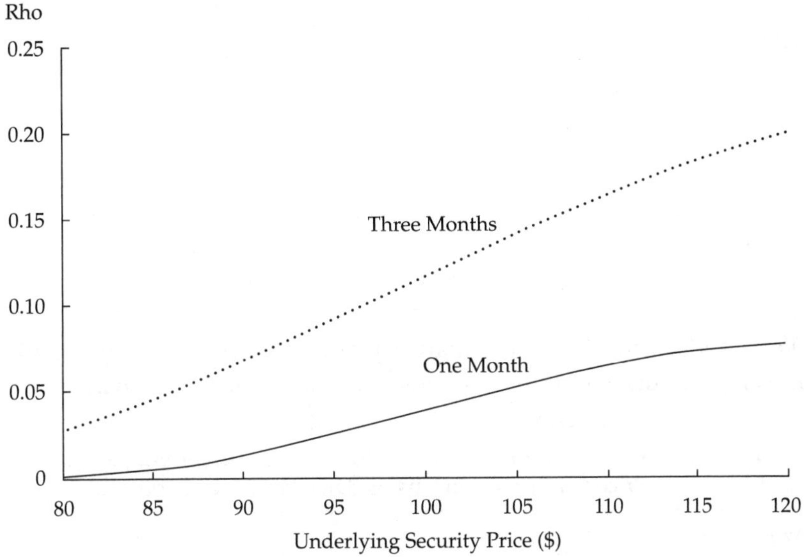

**Vega.** **Figure 6.9** plots the sensitivity of the option price to the volatility of the underlying security, or vega, which is the same value for both the call and put options. The figure shows that options are the most sensitive to changes in the volatility estimate when they are close to being at the money and in fact show little sensitivity to volatility when they are either far in or out of the money. For example, when a call option is deeply out of the money, the security price must move a lot before the call has any possibility of positive exercise value. Similarly, when the call option is deeply in the money, the underlying security price has to move a lot before the call would expire worthless. But when the underlying security price is close to the strike price, and the option is thus at the money, the volatility estimate is quite important and changes have a bigger impact on the value of the option because small movements in price will determine whether the option is in the money or not.

**Figure 6.9.    Relationship of Call and Put Vega to Underlying Security Price**

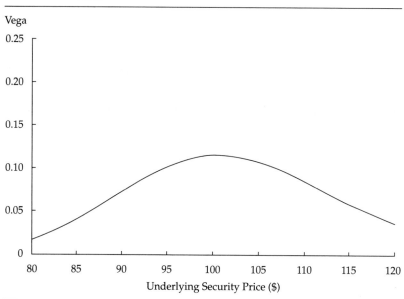

Vega is also sensitive to the maturity of the option, as shown in **Figure 6.10**. Long-maturity options are much more sensitive to changes in the

**Figure 6.10.    Relationship of Call and Put Vega to Underlying Security Price for Three Months vs. One Month to Expiration**

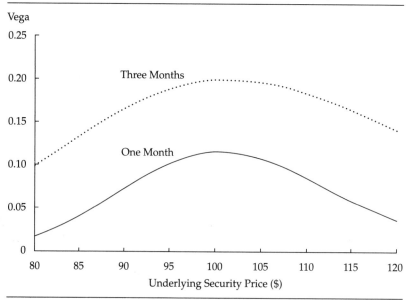

volatility estimate than are shorter-maturity options. For example, when at the money, a three-month option would increase in price by about 20 cents for a 1 percentage point increase in volatility, whereas a one-month option would increase by only about 11 cents.

## Risk Control Using Sensitivity Measures

The measures we have discussed describe the sensitivity of options to several parameters. An experienced investor would intuitively know the direction and approximate amount of risk associated with changes in market values, such as the underlying security price and volatility, but the greeks help quantify that risk and facilitate precise hedging strategies.

In terms of the size of the impact on option prices, the most crucial sensitivity measure is delta because other parameters tend to change more slowly than the underlying security price. Because delta is such a critical risk measure, gamma also plays an important role in measuring how rapidly delta might change as the security price changes. After delta and gamma, vega is perhaps the next most important sensitivity measure because the expected volatility of the underlying security can sometimes change rapidly, especially when the security price is changing rapidly. The expected volatility of the security is the only input to the Black–Scholes formula that is not directly observable. In fact, volatility is usually inferred from the option price itself by using a pricing model. Sensitivity of option prices to changes in interest rates, rho, receives less attention than delta and vega because interest rates generally change quite slowly, although interest rate changes are relatively more important for fixed-income derivatives.[2]

To illustrate the magnitude of the sensitivity measures and how they might be used in risk management, we provide numerical values in **Table 6.4** for call and put options at various strike prices and some basic option strategies. The values were calculated by using the Black–Scholes formula for options with one month to expiration when the underlying security price is $100, the interest rate is 2.00%, and volatility of the underlying security is 40.0%, similar to the prior numerical examples in this chapter. Using this set of parameters, we note that call options at lower strike prices have higher values and put options at lower strike prices have lower values. For example, the 90-strike call has the highest price, at $11.195, whereas the highest priced put option is the one with the 110 strike, at $11.242. Panel A of Table 6.4 provides the greeks for the five calls, and Panel B provides the greeks for the five puts. For example, the 100-strike call and put options have the same corresponding greek values as shown in Table 6.3.

---

[2]And, of course, time to expiration changes slowly over time, at a well-known constant rate!

**Table 6.4    Sample Sensitivity Measures**

| Position or Strategy | Price | Delta | Gamma | Theta | Rho | Vega |
|---|---|---|---|---|---|---|
| *A. Call option* | | | | | | |
| Call at X = 90 | 11.195 | 0.838 | 0.021 | −0.043 | 0.060 | 0.071 |
| Call at X = 95 | 7.527 | 0.697 | 0.030 | −0.063 | 0.052 | 0.101 |
| Call at X = 100 | 4.684 | 0.529 | 0.034 | −0.073 | 0.040 | 0.115 |
| Call at X = 105 | 2.689 | 0.363 | 0.032 | −0.069 | 0.028 | 0.108 |
| Call at X = 110 | 1.425 | 0.226 | 0.026 | −0.056 | 0.018 | 0.087 |
| *B. Put option* | | | | | | |
| Put at X = 90 | 1.045 | −0.162 | 0.021 | −0.038 | −0.014 | 0.071 |
| Put at X = 95 | 2.369 | −0.303 | 0.030 | −0.058 | −0.027 | 0.101 |
| Put at X = 100 | 4.517 | −0.471 | 0.034 | −0.067 | −0.043 | 0.115 |
| Put at X = 105 | 7.514 | −0.637 | 0.032 | −0.064 | −0.059 | 0.108 |
| Put at X = 110 | 11.242 | −0.774 | 0.026 | −0.050 | −0.074 | 0.087 |
| *C. Security and additional strategies* | | | | | | |
| Security | 100.000 | 1.000 | 0.000 | 0.000 | 0.000 | 0.000 |
| Covered call at 110 | 98.575 | 0.774 | −0.026 | 0.056 | −0.018 | −0.087 |
| Protective put at 90 | 101.045 | 0.838 | 0.021 | −0.038 | −0.014 | 0.071 |
| Straddle at 100 | 9.201 | 0.058 | 0.069 | −0.014 | −0.003 | 0.230 |
| Delta-neutral straddle, put ratio = 1.12 | 9.753 | 0.000 | 0.073 | −0.149 | −0.008 | 0.244 |
| Bull call spread at 95 and 105 | 4.838 | 0.334 | −0.002 | 0.007 | 0.024 | −0.008 |
| Vega-neutral bull call spread, call ratio = 0.93 | 5.025 | 0.359 | 0.000 | 0.002 | 0.026 | 0.000 |

*Note:* Values are calculated from the Black–Scholes model with parameter values of $S_0$ = $100, $T$ = 1/12 (30.4 days), $r$ = 2.00%, and σ = 40.0%.

Panel C of Table 6.4 lists the greeks for the underlying security, currently at $S_0$ = $100, and various option strategies. The security has a delta of exactly 1 and gamma of exactly 0 by definition, in that the price of the security always moves one-for-one with changes in itself. The sensitivity measures theta, rho, and vega are all 0, by definition, for the underlying security. The covered call position nets out the $1.425 price received for writing a 110-strike call option, for a total value of $98.575. Note that the delta of the covered call position is 1 minus the delta of the 110 call option, $1 - 0.226 = 0.774$, which is equal to the absolute value of the delta in the 110 put option because of put–call parity. Similarly, the price of the protective put position is $100 plus the price of a 90-strike put, $1.045, and the delta of the protective put at 90 is equal to the delta of 90-strike call.

Panel C of Table 6.4 also shows the values for an at-the-money straddle strategy, which includes the simultaneous purchase of a 100-strike call option and 100-strike put option, for a total cost of $4.684 + 4.517 = \$9.201$. The delta of the straddle is quite low, at $0.529 - 0.471 = 0.058$, meaning that the value is not very sensitive to movements up or down in the underlying security price. Indeed, the intent of a straddle strategy is to benefit from increases in volatility, as shown by the relatively high vega of 0.230, without making any significant bet on the *direction* of change in the underlying security price. Specifically, the vega of 0.230 indicates that a 1 percentage point increase in volatility, from 40% to 41%, will increase the value of the straddle position by 23.0 cents, a return of $0.230/9.201 = 2.50\%$. The straddle is known as a *long volatility strategy* because it increases in value with an increase in volatility.

The slightly positive value of the straddle's delta indicates it is not perfectly neutral to changes in the underlying security price, but that sensitivity can be strategically adjusted. In general, suppose an investor has a portfolio, $V$, consisting of one unit of Asset 1 and $h$ units of Asset 2, $V = A_1 + hA_2$. The change in the value of the portfolio as the security price changes is

$$\Delta_V = \Delta_1 + h\Delta_2, \tag{6.4}$$

where $\Delta$ is defined as a change in the value of an asset or portfolio resulting from a change in $S_0$. Solving for the hedge ratio in Equation 6.4 gives

$$h = \frac{\Delta_V - \Delta_1}{\Delta_2}. \tag{6.5}$$

A special case of hedging, called a *delta-neutral hedge*, occurs when the desired net delta of the portfolio is zero. To create a delta-neutral hedge, we set $\Delta_V$ equal to zero in Equation 6.5, which gives the hedge ratio:

$$h = -\frac{\Delta_1}{\Delta_2}. \tag{6.6}$$

In the straddle strategy, the first asset is the 100-strike call and the second asset is the 100-strike put, so a delta-neutral hedge can be constructed by buying $-0.529/-0.471 = 1.12$ puts for each call option. As shown in Table 6.4, the result of this modified straddle is an option strategy that remains long volatility, with a vega of 0.244 but a delta of exactly zero.

The delta of the call and put options are not constant, as evidenced by their nonzero gammas, so once the security price begins to change, the 1.12 put-to-call ratio might have to be adjusted to keep a delta-neutral position. To further mitigate against risk because of changes in the price of the underlying security, hedgers can also create positions that are both delta *and* gamma neutral.

The same measures of hedging can be applied to other option strategies. Table 6.4 contains a standard bull call spread created by buying a 95-strike call and selling a 105-strike call, for a total price of 7.527 − 2.689 = \$4.838. As intended, the bull call spread has a positive delta, meaning that the holder benefits from increases in the price of the underlying security. Specifically, the delta of 0.334 indicates that a \$1 increase in the underlying security price, from \$100 to \$101, will increase the spread value by 33.4 cents, a return of 0.334/4.838 = 6.90%. The −0.008 value of vega in the bull spread indicates some residual sensitivity to changes in security volatility even though the strategy includes buying one option and writing another.

As in the case of delta neutrality, to achieve a perfectly *vega-neutral* spread, we calculate the ratio of the vega values of the 95-strike call and 105-strike call, 0.101/0.108 = 0.93. Specifically, a bull call spread that writes 0.93 105-strike calls for every 95-strike call is perfectly vega neutral, as shown by the vega value of 0.000 in Table 6.4.

Portfolios of option positions can also be designed to be neutral to two sensitivity measures—for example, delta and gamma—at the same time. The strategy would need to include at least three (not two) separate positions, however, and the hedge ratio calculations would require a solution of two simultaneous equations, one for each of the neutrality conditions. Similarly, a portfolio of at least *four* option positions could be designed to be neutral to *three* sensitivity measures— say, delta, gamma, and vega—by solving three simultaneous equations.

One key concept here is that the delta of a strategy is simply the sum of the deltas of the individual positions within the strategy, and the same is true for vega and other sensitivity measures. Another important concept is that the *sensitivity measures are additive in their combined impact* on a single position. For example, the total change in a call option price as the various parameters change is

$$\Delta C = \left( \Delta_c + \frac{1}{2}\gamma_c \Delta S \right)\Delta S + \theta_c \Delta T + \rho_c \Delta r + v_c \Delta \sigma, \tag{6.7}$$

where
  $\Delta C$ = change in call option price
  $\Delta S$ = change in security price
  $\Delta T$ = change in time to expiration
  $\Delta r$ = change in interest rates
  $\Delta \sigma$ = change in volatility

Note that the impact of a change in the underlying security price is based on both the delta and gamma. For example, the call option in Table 6.3, with parameters $S_0 = \$100$, $X = \$100$, $T = 1/12$, $r = 2.00\%$, and $\sigma = 40.0\%$, has a price of $\$4.684$. Suppose that the underlying security price increases by $1, from $100 to $101, and that, at the same time, the volatility estimate drops 2 percentage points, from 40.0% to 38.0%. For simplicity, we will assume that no time has passed and that the interest rate remains unchanged. According to Equation 6.7, the combined impact of these parameter changes on the price of the call option is

$$\Delta C = \left[ 0.529 + \frac{1}{2} 0.034(1.00) \right] (1.00) - 0.073(0) + 0.040(0) + 0.115(-2)$$

$$= 0.316,$$

so the new price is 4.684 + 0.316 = \$5.000. The increase in the underlying security price, accounting for both the delta and gamma effects, would increase the call option price to $5.230, but the decrease in volatility offsets the movement in the security price somewhat, bringing the option price back down by 23.0 cents, to exactly $5.00, which results in a smaller net increase in the call option price.

## Alternative Ways to Create Option Effects

Call and put options are not always available for hedging a specific underlying security. Moreover, a particular option may be expensive (i.e., have a high implied volatility) or transaction costs may be prohibitive. So, methods for replicating option-like payoffs are useful. In this section, we discuss synthetic security creation based on the principle of put–call parity and then describe the process of dynamic hedging using only the underlying security to create option-like payoffs.

By moving the terms around, the basic European put–call parity relationship can be expressed in a number of different algebraic forms, but a common one that isolates the current price of the call option is

$$C_0 = S_0 + P_0 - \frac{X}{(1+r)^T}. \tag{6.8}$$

Equation 6.8 shows that the call option can be replicated by the underlying security plus the corresponding put option minus a cash-equivalent security or riskless bond. In other words, a *synthetic call option* can be created by buying the security and the put option, with most (although not all) of the cost covered by borrowing the present value of $X$. Specifically, the combination of securities on the right side of Equation 6.8 would produce the same risk–return payoff as buying the call option directly.

An alternative form of the put–call parity relationship,

$$P_0 = C_0 + \frac{X}{(1+r)^T} - S_0, \tag{6.9}$$

indicates that an investor can create a *synthetic put option* by buying the call option and investing the present value of $X$ at the risk-free rate, with most (although not all) of the cost covered by the proceeds from shorting the underlying security. Again, the combination of securities on the right side of Equation 6.9 would produce the same risk–return payoff as buying the put option directly.

In fact, the payoff of the underlying security itself can be replicated by buying a riskless bond with a face value of $X$, buying a call option, and writing a put option—according to another configuration of put–call parity,

$$S_0 = \frac{X}{(1+r)^T} + C_0 - P_0. \qquad (6.10)$$

In a similar way, a riskless bond can be constructed by buying the underlying security, buying a put option, and selling a call option.

We can also leave *two* terms on each side of the put–call parity formula to create a synthetic covered-call position:

$$S_0 - C_0 = \frac{X}{(1+r)^T} - P_0. \qquad (6.11)$$

On the left side of Equation 6.11, the traditional covered call position is established by buying the security and selling the call option, but the right side indicates that an equivalent position is to buy a riskless bond at a discount with a face value of $X$ and sell the put option.

Finally, a synthetic protective put can be created by buying a riskless bond at a discount with a face value of $X$ and buying a call option:

$$S_0 + P_0 = \frac{X}{(1+r)^T} + C_0. \qquad (6.12)$$

This configuration is often called a "90–10 strategy" because approximately 90% of the investor's capital is held in cash with 10% used to purchase call options.

Another way to create option-like effects is through dynamic hedging, the same process we used in Chapter 5 to justify the multiperiod binomial and the Black–Scholes option-pricing models. In its most general form, dynamic hedging requires a replicating portfolio, $R$, with positions in the underlying security, $S_0$, and a riskless bond or cash-equivalent security, $B$:

$$R = (w)S_0 + (1-w)B, \qquad (6.13)$$

where $w$ is the proportion of the replicating portfolio invested in the underlying security. The change in replicating portfolio value for a change in the price of the underlying security is

$$\Delta R = (w)1 + (1-w)0$$
$$= w, \qquad (6.14)$$

so the process of dynamic hedging requires that the investor keep the proportion of the portfolio invested in the underlying security, $w$, equal to the delta of the strategy to be replicated.

Suppose, for example, that an investor is concerned about price declines and wants to replicate a protective put. The investor knows that according to put–call parity, the delta of a protective put is equal to the delta of the corresponding call, a number between 0 and 1, depending on the moneyness of the call and the other option parameters. For instance, suppose the underlying security is a stock priced at $100, as in Table 6.4, and the investor wants to replicate the value of a one-month protective put at $95. The delta of the protective put strategy is 0.697 (1.0 − 0.303), so the investor with $100,000 to hedge buys 697 shares at $100 each and invests the remaining $30,300 in a cash account. If the price of the stock falls, the investor incurs only a partial loss, similar to the loss incurred if the entire $100,000 were invested in a protective put strategy. But as the price declines, the investor needs to reduce the proportion of the replicating portfolio invested in stocks to maintain a delta hedge equal to a protective put strategy. Specifically, the delta of the protective put strategy decreases with declines in the stock price, according to the gamma value of 0.030 in Table 6.4. Thus, for a $1 decline in the stock price, the investor needs to sell about 30 shares to reduce the replicating portfolio's delta to match the new delta of the protective put strategy, leaving 697 − 30 = 667 shares. If the stock price increases by $1, the protective put replicator needs to buy 30 more shares using cash in the portfolio. This approach is the classic put replication strategy used by so-called portfolio insurance providers.

As with arbitrage-free option pricing itself, option strategy replication through dynamic hedging assumes relatively smooth changes in the underlying security price with no large or sudden jumps. This assumption may not always hold, as users of portfolio insurance strategies found out in the October 1987 equity market crash. Moreover, the continual buying and selling of shares to maintain a nearly perfect hedge involves high transaction costs. Because buying and selling the actual underlying security—for example, the S&P 500 Index portfolio—could be prohibitively expensive, investors sometimes substitute futures contracts for the underlying security, thus reducing transaction costs and increasing the speed of execution.

## Implied Volatility Smiles and Term Structure

The existence of option contracts for a range of strike prices on an underlying security allows option analysts to measure aspects of the probability distribution that are not directly observable without option markets. Similarly, option contracts with different times to expiration can be used to forecast how the volatility of the underlying security is expected to evolve over time. Both the detailed probability distribution and the term structure of volatility perspectives use the concept of implied volatility, defined as the volatility parameter that justifies a quoted option price.

For example, **Table 6.5** shows September call option quotes for a range of strike prices for Apple Inc. (AAPL) shares on Friday, 11 August 2012, when AAPL closed at $621.70. Each quote yields an implied volatility, backed out of the Black–Scholes formula with $T = 0.100$ (approximately five weeks) and $r = 0.20\%$. Note that Apple will not pay a dividend prior to the September expiration date, so these American-style options can be reasonably valued by using the European-style Black–Scholes formula. Under a lognormal probability distribution, as was originally assumed in the Black–Scholes model, the implied volatilities are assumed to be equal for all strike prices in the table.

However, the volatilities implied by the option quotes in Table 6.5 decrease from 26.75% for the deeply in-the-money 560-strike call to 20.83% for the out-of-the-money 660-strike call. The pattern indicates a skewed probability distribution for AAPL returns—a fat left tail compared with the more symmetrical lognormal distribution. Interestingly, the implied volatility does increase slightly with the more deeply out-of-the-money 680-call, suggesting that the right tail of the probability distribution may also be a little fat.

Table 6.5    Implied Volatilities of AAPL at Various Strike Prices, 11 August 2012

| Strike | Call Price Quote ($) | Implied Volatility (%) |
|---|---|---|
| 560 | 64.40 | 26.75 |
| 580 | 46.50 | 24.51 |
| 600 | 30.55 | 22.75 |
| 620 | 17.95 | 21.74 |
| 640 | 9.25 | 21.11 |
| 660 | 4.20 | 20.83 |
| 680 | 1.85 | 21.22 |

When the implied volatilities are plotted against the strike price, as in **Figure 6.11**, the curve forms what analysts call a *smile* (if the curve is symmetrical) or, in this case, a *smirk* because there is only a little increase in volatility on the right side of the chart. Many large-cap individual stocks in the equity market exhibit this kind of skewed left tail, suggesting that the implied return probability distributions are routinely nonnormal.

**Figure 6.11.    Implied Volatilities from AAPL Call Options**

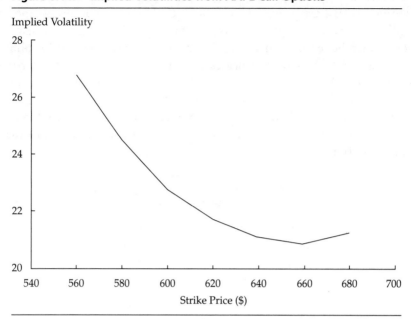

A similar kind of implied volatility analysis can also be conducted by using different option maturity dates instead of different strike prices. These time-series versus cross-sectional implied volatility calculations allow analysts to examine what is sometimes considered the *term structure* of risk in the underlying security. For example, on the same date as in Table 6.5, the price quote for the October (rather than September) 620-strike-price call option for Apple shares was $26.65. The volatility implied by this price quote adjusted for the longer time to expiration in the Black–Scholes formula was 24.71% instead of 21.74%. The volatility implied by the even further out November 620-strike call option adjusted for the even longer time to expiration and the early November quarterly dividend for Apple was even higher, 27.13%. These implied volatility calculations suggest that the risk of the underlying security—in this case, Apple shares—was forecasted by investors to increase over the next few months, as was the risk of most large-cap domestic stocks in early August 2012.

The volatility implied from options on market indices, in addition to index levels themselves, are now routinely provided as market indicators. For example, VIX, the Market Volatility Index for the Chicago Board Options Exchange, is the volatility implied by the price of options on the S&P 500. As of the close of trading on 20 August 2012, the CBOE quoted the VIX as 14.30, meaning the annualized volatility of the S&P 500 implied by the various option prices with September (one-month) expiration was 14.30%. The

VIX quotes for September and longer-maturity option expiration dates as of mid-August 2012 are provided in **Table 6.6**. Although not always the case, the VIX quotes are higher for longer-term expiration dates—for example, 16.45 for October expiration and 19.76 for December (five-month) expiration. The pattern of VIX quotes indicates that in August 2012, market participants expected the volatility of the S&P 500 to be lower over the next month than further in the future. The near-term VIX was more than 30% in August 2011, when the market had recently experienced considerable turbulence, and the term structure was downward sloping, with lower values for more distant option expiration dates.

**Table 6.6    VIX at Various Expiration Dates, as of Mid-August 2012**

| Expiration Month | Quote |
|---|---|
| September (near term) | 14.30 |
| October | 16.45 |
| November | 18.29 |
| December | 19.76 |
| December 2013 | 24.75 |
| December 2014 | 26.81 |

## Conclusion

Options and futures have many similarities in terms of their ability to manage the risk of investment positions and to create market exposure synthetically. The fundamental hedging principles are the same, but the asymmetry inherent in options makes hedging with options more complex and creates opportunities not generally available with futures contracts. Short-term hedging using options involves a number of sensitivity parameters, including delta, which measures the sensitivity of the option price to a change in the underlying security price. Quoted option prices provide a measure of underlying security volatility that can be used to value other options on the same security and to forecast future volatility. In summary, both option and futures contracts can be important tools for managing investment risk, but the specific pricing structures and applications differ considerably between options and futures.

# Appendix. Interest Rate Concepts

The use of fixed-income derivatives—for example, U.S. Treasury bond futures—requires some background in basic interest rate concepts. This appendix reviews three topics concerning interest rates and fixed-income securities that are relevant to using fixed-income derivatives: simple versus compound interest rate quotations, the term structure of interest rates, and measuring the interest rate risk of bonds using duration, convexity, and DV01—the dollar value of a 1 bp change in the interest rate.

## Interest Rate Quotations

Investors generally think in terms of *annualized* interest rates, but interest rates over a shorter period are annualized in financial mathematics in at least two distinct ways—simple interest and compound interest. For example, monthly interest earned on a certificate of deposit or paid on a mortgage at a commercial bank is annualized by using a simple interest calculation. Specifically, if a customer earns 20 bps per month on the balance in a savings account, the bank might quote an annualized percentage rate of 12 × 20 bps = 2.40%. This simple interest calculation does not account for the interest earned each month on the interest from prior months, the effect of compounding. In fact, the *effective annual rate* (EAR) of return, or *compound interest* over the year, in this numerical example is $(1 + 0.0020)^{12} - 1 = 2.43\%$, meaning that for $100 invested at the beginning of the year, the account will actually contain $102.43 at the end of the year, not $102.40.

At the current (spring 2012) low interest rates that prevail in many developed economies, the difference in numerical values between quoting conventions may be small, but it is still conceptually important. Although we do not cover all of the various quoting conventions here, we will mention a few that are common in dealing with fixed-income derivatives: money market yield (for euro deposits), discount rate basis (for Treasury bills), and bond-equivalent yield (for bonds and notes). The rates quoted in these various fixed-income markets can be compared with each other by converting them to a common basis—the effective annual rate that measures the true increase in dollar value. We will also mention the idea of *continuously compounded rates of return*, which are often used in option-pricing models.

The annualized *money market yield* is a simple interest rate, $r$, quoted with the twist that the number of periods is based on a 360-day year divided by the number of days over which interest is paid. The dollars of interest paid over $t$

days is divided by the initial dollars of principal and then multiplied by 360 over *t*:

$$r = \frac{\text{Interest}}{\text{Principal}}\left(\frac{360}{t}\right). \tag{A.1}$$

So, for example, if interest of \$0.20 is paid on principal of \$100 after 10 days, the quoted money market rate would be

$$r = \frac{0.20}{100.00}\left(\frac{360}{10}\right)$$

$$= 7.20\%.$$

The EAR, which better reflects the economic reality of the gain, would be

$$\text{EAR} = \left(1 + \frac{0.20}{100.00}\right)^{365/10} - 1$$

$$= 7.57\%.$$

T-bills, which are purchased at a discount to face value, do not pay interest directly. They are quoted on a *bank discount rate* basis and also use the convention of a 360-day year. The bank discount rate is not a true return calculation, in that the investor's gain, or dollar difference between the purchase price and face value payoff, is divided by the final, rather than the initial, cash flow. Specifically, the dollars of discount from the face value are divided by face value and then multiplied by 360 over *t* days:

$$d = \frac{\text{Discount}}{\text{Face value}}\left(\frac{360}{t}\right). \tag{A.2}$$

For example, if a T-bill with 20 days to maturity and a face value of \$1,000 is selling for \$996, the rate quoted on a bank discount basis is

$$d = \frac{4}{1,000}\left(\frac{360}{20}\right)$$

$$= 7.20\%,$$

whereas the EAR would be

$$\text{EAR} = \left(1 + \frac{4}{996}\right)^{365/20} - 1$$

$$= 7.59\%.$$

The yield on T-bonds, which pay interest every six months, is a simple interest rate calculation in that the semiannual yield, or interest payment divided by price, is simply doubled to arrive at the *bond-equivalent yield*:

$$y = \frac{\text{Coupon}}{\text{Price}}(2). \tag{A.3}$$

Thus, the only distinction between the bond-equivalent yield and EAR is simple versus compound interest. Specifically, if a $1,000 face value T-bond has exactly six months to maturity and pays a coupon of $36, the bond equivalent yield is

$$y = \frac{36}{1000}\,(2)$$
$$= 7.20\%.$$

whereas the EAR is

$$EAR = \left(1 + \frac{36}{1000}\right)^2 - 1$$
$$= 7.33\%.$$

The continuously compounded rates in option models, such as the Black–Scholes formula, use continuous time mathematics. The notion of a continuously compounded rate can be illustrated by increasing the frequency of compounding—that is, using shorter and shorter periods. For example, the bond-equivalent yield of 7.20% led to a 7.33% EAR because of semiannual compounding. If a commercial bank advertised a 7.20% savings rate compounded *monthly*, the EAR would be

$$EAR = \left(1 + \frac{0.0720}{12}\right)^{12} - 1 = 7.44\%,$$

and with *daily* compounding, it would be 2 bps higher, at

$$EAR = \left(1 + \frac{0.0720}{365}\right)^{365} - 1 = 7.46\%.$$

The extension to continuous time uses natural logs [Excel function LN()] and the exponents of the natural number $e = 2.17828$ [Excel function EXP()]. Specifically, the relationship between a continuously compounded rate $c$ and the EAR is given by

$$EAR = e^c - 1, \tag{A.4}$$

so a 7.20% annual percentage continuously compounded has an EAR of

$$EAR = e^{0.0720} - 1 = 7.47\%,$$

which is only 1 bp higher than with daily compounding.

The inverse function, to translate an EAR into a continuously compounded rate, is given by

$$c = \ln(1 + EAR). \tag{A.5}$$

For example, the risk-free rate parameter in the Black–Scholes formula reviewed in Chapter 5 is a continuous rate, which will be slightly lower than the effective annual rate or actual economic gain over a year, as calculated in standard "discrete time" financial mathematics.

## The Term Structure of Interest Rates

The *term structure of interest rates* describes the annualized rate or yield offered by fixed-income securities across various maturities, all measured at one point in time. When these yields are plotted against time to maturity, from short term to long term, the resulting figure is called a *yield curve*. A flat yield curve indicates that short-term interest rates are currently equal to long-term interest rates. For most of the 20th century, the U.S. dollar yield curve has been upward sloping, meaning that long-term interest rates were higher than short-term rates. But this was not always the case. For example, the yield curve for Treasury securities was downward sloping in the early 1980s, when short-term interest rates were higher than long-term rates. As of the writing of this book, interest rates for most developed countries are quite low by historical standards, but the yield curves are still upward sloping. For example, **Figure A.1** plots the yield on U.K.

**Figure A.1.    U.K. (British Pound) Yield Curve**

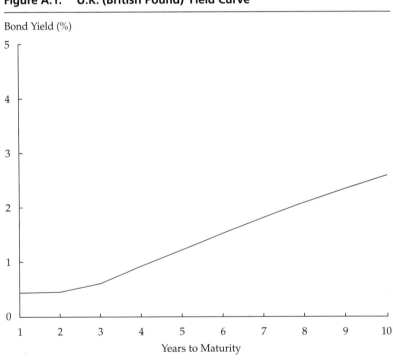

government bonds with maturities from 1 year to 10 years as of March 2012. Note that, although for most of this book, we use U.S. financial market examples and currency, we are using a non-U.S. bond in this example because the coupons are paid annually. The semiannual coupons and associated bond-equivalent yield of U.S. Treasury securities complicate the numerical examples and intuition.

One of the reasons for an upward-sloping yield curve might be that holders of long-term bonds require a risk premium reflecting uncertainty about the path of future interest rates. Markets often manifest an upward-sloping yield curve, suggesting a gradual increase in short-term rates in the future. For example, suppose the current one-year interest rate (yield on a one-year, zero-coupon, risk-free bond) is 2% and that market participants expect that the yield on a one-year bond one year from now will be 4% and that the one-year yield on a one-year bond two years from now will be 6%. What will the price and yield of a two-year bond be right now with those expectations? Using basic time-value-of-money financial mathematics, an analyst will find that the current price of a two-year bond with a face value of 100 is

$$\frac{100}{(1+0.02)(1+0.04)} = 94.27$$

and the annualized yield based on this price is

$$\left(\frac{100.00}{94.27}\right)^{1/2} - 1 = 3.00\%.$$

Similarly, the current price of a three-year bond with a face value of 100 is

$$\frac{100}{(1+0.02)(1+0.04)(1+0.06)} = 88.93,$$

and the annualized yield based on this price is

$$\left(\frac{100.00}{88.93}\right)^{1/3} - 1 = 3.99\%.$$

In this numerical example, a yield curve would plot *spot rates* of 2.00%, 3.00%, and 3.99% (almost 4%), for, respectively, the one-year, two-year, and three-year maturity bonds. Even if analysts did not know the underlying short-term interest rates of 2%, 4%, and 6%, they could easily infer from the shape of the yield curve that *short rates* in the future were expected to be higher.

In fact, given two successive spot rates, we can calculate the *forward rate* as a forecast of the future short-term interest rate implied by the yield curve. Intuitively, the annualized interest rate over two years would be the average of the first and second year, so if the first year is 2% and the average is almost 3%, then the second year must be about 4%. Similarly, an average of three numbers of almost 4%, where the first two numbers are 2% and 4%, implies that the third number is about 6%. These arithmetic averages are not exact because rates of return are multiplicative, but the intuition is fairly straightforward.

We will use the following terminology, with associated mathematical notation, in the context of more exact term structure analysis.

| Terminology | Notation | Definition |
|---|---|---|
| Short rate | $r_t$ | Short-term interest rate over period $t$ (e.g., year) |
| Spot rate | $y_t$ | Yield on a bond that matures at the end of period $t$ |
| Forward rate | $f_t$ | The future short-term interest rate over period $t$ implied by two successive spot rates |

The word *short* in this context comes from the idea of short-term rates, and the word *spot* implies right now, as opposed to a rate that might occur in the future. The phrase *pure spot rate* emphasizes that the bonds in question are zero-coupon bonds, so the annualized yield is uncontaminated by the impact of interim cash flows. The phrase *implied forward rate* emphasizes that the forward rate is a calculated value that is implied by the spot rates.

The exact algebraic relationships that account for the multiplicative nature of returns can be derived from the time-value-of-money mathematics. Specifically, a multiperiod spot rate (yield on a zero-coupon bond) is a function of the short-term interest rates that will prevail over the life of the bond:

$$y_t = \left[(1+r_1)(1+r_2)\dots(1+r_t)\right]^{1/t} - 1. \tag{A.6}$$

More importantly, a forecast of the short-term interest rate that will prevail over a future period $t$ can be inferred from two successive spot rates in the current market:

$$f_t = \frac{(1+y_t)^t}{(1+y_{t-1})^{t-1}} - 1. \tag{A.7}$$

Because the short-term rates that will eventually prevail in the marketplace are not known before the fact, the forward rate is typically used by analysts as a forecast or expected value of the eventual short rate:

$$f_t = E(r_t). \tag{A.8}$$

The actual short rate realized after the fact, $r_t$, might end up being above or below the analysts forecast, $f_t$, but the calculation and concept of forward rates is important in many fixed-income applications, including hedging with derivatives.

**Table A.1** illustrates the calculation of pure spot rates and forward rates for U.K. government bonds in March 2012. The annual coupon rate and yield

**Table A1.    U.K. Bond Spot and Forward Rates in March 2012**

| Years to Maturity | Coupon Rate | Yield to Maturity | Price | Spot Rate, $y$ | Forward Rate, $f$ |
|---|---|---|---|---|---|
| 1 | 4.50% | 0.44% | 104.042 | 0.440% | |
| 2 | 2.25 | 0.47 | 103.535 | 0.470 | 0.501% |
| 3 | 2.75 | 0.62 | 106.312 | 0.624 | 0.933 |
| 4 | 2.00 | 0.93 | 104.182 | 0.942 | 1.900 |
| 5 | 1.75 | 1.21 | 102.605 | 1.228 | 2.382 |
| 6 | 5.00 | 1.47 | 120.132 | 1.545 | 3.143 |
| 7 | 4.50 | 1.73 | 118.115 | 1.823 | 3.507 |
| 8 | 4.75 | 1.98 | 120.309 | 2.108 | 4.126 |
| 9 | 3.75 | 2.23 | 112.272 | 2.360 | 4.399 |
| 10 | 4.00 | 2.42 | 113.886 | 2.582 | 4.602 |

to maturity of the bonds in the first two columns are inputs to the bond price calculations in the third column in standard time-value-of-money functions. More complex calculation procedures (not covered here) could determine the *pure* spot rates, defined as the yield that would prevail on a zero-coupon bond at each maturity. Note that the spot rates, $y_t$, are close but not exactly equal to the coupon bond yields, which are a complex average of the spot rates over the life of the bond. The forward rate, $f$, at each maturity is calculated from the current and prior spot rate, $y_t$ and $y_{t-1}$, by using Equation A.7. For example, the short-term interest rate in the United Kingdom was 0.440% in March 2012 and the one-year forward rate is slightly higher, at 0.501%. The term structure of interest rates indicates that one-year forward rates increase quickly after the second year and rise as high as 4.602% at the beginning of the tenth year.

## Measuring Interest Rate Risk

The price of long-term fixed-income securities changes as interest rates change, and being able to describe how the price will change is important for those trying to hedge with derivatives. Duration and convexity are two measures of interest rate risk that help describe how the price of the bond will change as its yield to maturity changes. **Figure A.2** plots how the price of a bond changes with changes in yield. Note that bond prices decrease with higher yield and increase with lower yield, although the function is curved rather than linear. *Duration* provides a measure of the slope of the curve at a given price and yield, as shown by the dotted line tangent at a given point on the curve in Figure A.2. *Convexity* is a measure that helps correct the

**Figure A.2.  Bond Price as a Function of Yield**

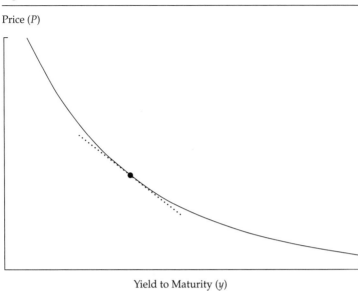

Price (P)

Yield to Maturity (y)

linear extrapolation of a bond price back to a more accurate price based on the degree of curvature in the price–yield curve.

Frederick Macaulay (1910) coined the term *duration* in the early 20th century for the weighted average time to payment of a security's cash flows, where the weights in the averaging process are based on the present value of each cash flow over the total price. For example, a bond with a 10-year maturity and fixed coupons might have an average time to payment of about 8 years, where the average puts more weight on the payment of principal in the 10th year than the smaller coupon payments in Years 1–9. Using calculus, we can show that this calculation of average time to maturity is equivalent to the negative of the change in bond price for a given change in yield. The most commonly used form of duration is *modified duration*, defined as the percentage change in price for a change in yield:

$$D^* = \frac{\Delta P / P}{\Delta y}$$

$$= \frac{\%\Delta P}{\Delta y}.$$

(A.9)

The asterisk notation differentiates modified duration from Macaulay duration, $D$. Specifically, modified duration is equal to the Macaulay duration (i.e., average time to maturity) divided by 1 plus the yield,

$$D^* = \frac{D}{(1 + y)}.$$

(A.10)

The first three columns of **Table A.2** provide a detailed calculation of the price of a 10-year bond with annual coupon of 4% and priced to yield 5%.

The bond price of 92.28 shown at the bottom of the third column of Table A.2 is simply the sum of the present values of the cash flows:

$$P = \sum_{t=1}^{T} \frac{CF_t}{(1+y)^t}. \tag{A.11}$$

The price of a fixed-coupon bond expressed as a percentage of par or face value has a somewhat intuitive closed-form (i.e., without summations) formula:

$$p = \frac{c}{y}\left[1 - \frac{1}{(1+y)^T}\right] + \frac{1}{(1+y)^T}, \tag{A.12}$$

where

$c$ = coupon rate

$y$ = yield

$T$ = number of periods to maturity

The first term in Equation A.12 captures the present value of the coupons, and the second term captures the present value of the eventual face value payment. For example, the bond in Table A.2 has a price relative to par of

$$p = \frac{0.04}{0.05}\left[1 - \frac{1}{(1+0.05)^{10}}\right] + \frac{1}{(1+0.05)^{10}} = 0.9228,$$

**Table A2. Duration and Convexity Calculations**

| $t$ | $CF_t$ | $PV(CF_t)$ | $w_t = PV(CF_t)/P$ | $w_t^* t$ | $w_t^* t^* (t+1)$ |
|---|---|---|---|---|---|
| 1 | 4.00 | 3.81 | 4.13% | 0.04 | 0.08 |
| 2 | 4.00 | 3.63 | 3.93 | 0.08 | 0.24 |
| 3 | 4.00 | 3.46 | 3.74 | 0.11 | 0.45 |
| 4 | 4.00 | 3.29 | 3.57 | 0.14 | 0.71 |
| 5 | 4.00 | 3.13 | 3.40 | 0.17 | 1.02 |
| 6 | 4.00 | 2.98 | 3.23 | 0.19 | 1.36 |
| 7 | 4.00 | 2.84 | 3.08 | 0.22 | 1.73 |
| 8 | 4.00 | 2.71 | 2.93 | 0.23 | 2.11 |
| 9 | 4.00 | 2.58 | 2.79 | 0.25 | 2.51 |
| 10 | 104.00 | 63.85 | 69.19 | 6.92 | 76.11 |
| Sums | | 92.28 | 100.00% | 8.36 | 86.32 |

*Notes: $CF_t$ stands for cash flow at time $t$, PV stands for present value, and $w_t$ stands for weight for time $t$. The sums in the last two columns are for Macaulay duration and convexity. Using Equations A.10 and A.15, we can calculate the modified duration and convexity, respectively, as 7.96 and 78.29.*

or 92.28%. If coupons are paid semiannually and yield is quoted as twice the semiannual rate, as is the case for most bonds in the United States, then appropriate adjustments (doubling or halving) must be made to the variables—for example,

$$p = \frac{0.020}{0.025}\left[1 - \frac{1}{(1+0.025)^{20}}\right] + \frac{1}{(1+0.025)^{20}}$$

$$= 0.9221.$$

For simplicity and intuition, we will continue to discuss bonds for which the underlying interest payment period is annual.

The fourth column in Table A.2 calculates weights based on the present values of each cash flow, and the fifth column calculates the Macaulay duration, defined as the weighted average time to maturity of the bond,

$$D = \sum_{t=1}^{T}\left[\frac{CF_t}{P(1+y)^t}\right]t$$

$$= \sum_{t=1}^{T} w_t\, t,$$

$$= 8.36,$$

(A.13)

a duration of $D = 8.36$ years. The modified duration calculation requires one more step,

$$D^* = \frac{D}{(1+y)}$$

$$= \frac{8.36}{(1+0.05)}$$

$$= 7.96,$$

a modified duration of $D^* = 7.96$ years. Modified duration also has a closed-form formula for a fixed-coupon bond,

$$D^* = \frac{1}{y} - \frac{1 + T\left[(c-y)/(1+y)\right]}{c\left[(1+y)^T - 1\right] + y}.$$

(A.14)

For example, using the parameter values of the bond in Table A.2 gives

$$D^* = \frac{1}{0.05} - \frac{1 + 10\left[(0.04-0.05)/(1+0.05)\right]}{0.04\left[(1+0.05)^{10} - 1\right] + 0.05} = 7.96,$$

or, again, $D^* = 7.96$ years.

In application, modified duration (hereafter simply *duration*) is not so much a measure of time but of the price sensitivity of the bond to changes in interest rates or yield, as noted in Equation A.9. For example, if the yield on the bond in Table A.2 goes down by 10 bps, the duration of 7.96 indicates that the approximate percentage increase in price will be –7.96 × (–10) = 79.6 bps. Similarly, if the yield drops by 20 bps, the duration of 7.96 indicates that the approximate percentage increase in price will be –7.96 × (–20) = 159.2 bps. Note that duration in this context is used as a simple multiplier against the yield change, with a leading negative sign because bond prices move in the opposite direction from a change in yield.

As shown by the dotted line in Figure A.2, duration is a linear extrapolation based on the slope of the convex price–yield curve at a given point. As a result, the estimated price change based on duration is only approximate, and the error is bigger for larger changes in yield. For example, if the yield on the bond in Table A.2 increases by 100 bps, from 5.00% to 6.00%, the estimated percentage price change will be –7.96 × 100 = –796 bps, or –7.96 percentage points. But if Equation A.12 is used, the actual price of the bond at the new 6.00% yield is 85.28, a –7.58 percentage point change.

To provide a more accurate representation of the interest rate risk in bond prices, analysts also use the notion of *convexity*, based on a second derivative in calculus. As shown in the last column of Table A.2, convexity can be calculated by the summation

$$C = \sum_{t=1}^{T} \left[ \frac{CF_t}{P(1+y)^t} \right] t\,(t+1)$$

$$= \sum_{t=1}^{T} w_t\, t\,(t+1),$$

(A.15)

which gives $C = 86.32$ as shown at the bottom of Table A.2.

Similar to duration, the convention is to modify convexity by dividing by 1 plus the yield squared,

$$C^* = \frac{C}{(1+y)^2} = \frac{86.32}{(1+.05)^2} = 78.29.$$

Modified convexity (hereafter simply *convexity*) does not have an intuitive unit of measure. Although closed-form formulas for the convexity of fixed-coupon bonds exist, they are complex and have little intuitive value or conceptual interpretation. Convexity is used to obtain a more exact description of the impact of changes in yield on the percentage change in price by using the Taylor-series expansion formula:

$$\frac{\Delta P}{P} = -D^*(\Delta y) + \frac{C^*(\Delta y)^2}{2}.$$

(A.16)

For example, the estimated percentage change in the price of the bond in Table A.2 for a 100 bps increase in yield when *both* duration and convexity are used is

$$\frac{\Delta P}{P} = -7.96(0.0100) + \frac{78.29(0.0100)^2}{2}$$

$$= -7.57\%,$$

which is quite close to the previously discussed actual price change of −7.58%.

To some extent, the motivation for the original mathematics of duration and convexity has disappeared because computer technology allows one to calculate the actual price impacts of any interest rate change, but the language and concepts associated with these two risk measures are deeply embedded in fixed-income analysis and, therefore, the analysis of derivative securities. For example, the "duration" of a bond futures contract may change suddenly, rather than gradually, as different cheapest-to-deliver (CTD) bonds become the best way to fulfill the contract. Or consider another example: A callable bond in which the upper portion of the price curve that would be displayed in Figure A.1 is concave instead of convex is said to exhibit "negative convexity," in that duration for it decreases rather than increases as interest rates increase.

Although a futures contract on a bond does not have a series of cash flows over time like the underlying note or bond, the interest rate sensitivity or effective duration can be derived from its relationship to the CTD security. Using the equation for the fair value of a futures contract on a bond given in Chapter 2, Equation 2.5, we find the duration of the futures contract with price $F_0$ and CTD bond price $P_{CTD}$ to be

$$D_F^* = D_{CTD}^* \left[ \frac{P_{CTD}}{f\,F_0} \right] (1+r)^t, \tag{A.17}$$

where
   $f$ = delivery or conversion factor of the CTD note or bond
   $r$ = short-term risk-free rate
   $t$ = time to futures contract expiration

Note that the effective duration of the futures contract is related to the duration of the CTD bond. The term $(1 + r)^t$ is often dropped in the calculation because it is close to 1 for a near-term futures contract.

If the investor were trying to hedge the interest rate risk of a bond with price $P_B$ and duration $D_B^*$, the hedge ratio would include the change in yield on that bond, $\Delta y_B$, relative to the change in yield of the CTD bond, $\Delta y_{CTD}$:

$$h = -\frac{D_B^*}{D_F^*}\left(\frac{P_B}{F_0}\right)\left(\frac{\Delta y_B}{\Delta y_{CTD}}\right). \tag{A.18}$$

The two yield changes are often assumed to be equal, so the last term would be equal to 1. Combining Equations A.17 and A.18 allows us to calculate the hedge ratio by using values for the bond to be hedged and the CTD bond:

$$h = -\frac{D_B^*}{D_{CTD}^*}\left(\frac{fP_B}{P_{CTD}}\right)\frac{1}{(1+r)^t}\left(\frac{\Delta y_B}{\Delta y_{CTD}}\right), \tag{A.19}$$

where, again, the last two terms are often assumed to be 1.

The dollar value change in a bond's price for a 1 bp change in a bond's yield—that is, DV01—is closely related to the bond's duration. Specifically, modified duration is multiplied by bond price and by 0.0001 (i.e., 1 bp) so that the price change is in dollars rather than a percentage:

$$DV01 = D_B^* P_B (0.0001). \tag{A.20}$$

For example, the DV01 for a bond priced at \$1,000 with a modified duration of 5.0 is

$$DV01 = 5.0(1,000)(0.0001)$$
$$= \$0.50.$$

Thus, the DV01 can be used instead of duration to calculate the price impact of a change in yield, measured in basis points:

$$\Delta P_B = -DV01(\Delta y_B). \tag{A.21}$$

For example, a 10 bp drop in the yield on the example bond would increase the price by

$$\Delta P_B = -\$0.50(-10) = \$5.00,$$

or 0.5% of the initial \$1,000 bond price, for a new price of \$1,005.

Similarly, the DV01 for a futures contract is based on the futures duration and the futures price:

$$DV01_F = D_F^* F_0 (0.0001). \tag{A.22}$$

Finally, substituting Equation A.17 for the duration of a futures contract into Equation A.22 gives a relationship between the futures DV01 and the DV01 of the CTD bond as

$$DV01_F = \frac{D_{CTD}^* P_{CTD}(0.0001)}{f}(1+r)^t = \frac{DV01_{CDT}}{f}(1+r)^t, \tag{A.23}$$

where the last term is often assumed to be 1.

# Exercises

## Futures Pricing

### Exercise 1

Calculate the fair value of the following contracts with 25 trading days ($t = 25/250 = 0.10$ years) to expiration and an effective annualized risk-free interest rate of 1.5% for the 25-day period:

a. An equity index futures contract with the current index level of 1,364.10 and an annualized dividend yield of 2.1%.

b. A foreign exchange futures contract for British pounds with the current spot price of USD1.620/GBP and the foreign risk-free interest rate of 2.6%.

c. A U.S. Treasury bond futures contract with the market price of the cheapest-to-deliver (CTD) bond equal to 84 16/32 (84.500). The CTD bond has a coupon rate of 5.0%, accrued interest of 0.375, and a delivery factor of 0.9140.

### Solutions

a. The fair value of the equity futures contract is

$$F_0 = S_0(1+r-d)^t = 1,364.10(1+0.015-0.021)^{0.10} = 1,363.28.$$

The futures price is slightly lower than the spot price because the dividend yield of the underlying index is higher than the interest rate.

b. The fair value for the foreign exchange futures contract is

$$F_0 = S_0 \left(\frac{1+r_d}{1+r_f}\right)^t = 1.620\left(\frac{1+0.015}{1+0.026}\right)^{0.10} = 1.618.$$

c. The fair value of the T-bond futures contract is

$$F_0 = \frac{(S_0 + AI)(1+r)^t}{f} = \frac{(84.500+0.375)(1+0.015)^{0.10}}{0.9140} = 92.999,$$

where $AI$ is the accrued interest adjustment.

# Implied Repo Rates

### Exercise 2

Calculate the implied repo rate if the actual market price of the equity futures contract in Exercise 1a were 1,366.70. How would an investor construct an arbitrage position to earn this rate of return?

#### Solution

The futures contract implied repo rate can be found by rewriting the relationship as

$$r = \left(\frac{F_0}{S_0}\right)^{1/t} + d - 1$$

$$= \left(\frac{1,366.7}{1,364.1}\right)^{10} + 0.021 - 1$$

$$= 4.0\%.$$

The arbitrage position would require buying a basket of stocks to replicate the S&P 500 Index and selling the futures contract. At the expiration of the contract, the investor would have earned an annualized 4.0% minus any transaction costs to construct the portfolio. Tracking error between the physical stocks and the index would add some variability to the arbitrage return.

### Exercise 3

Calculate the implied domestic repo rate if the futures price in Exercise 1b were equal to USD1.630/GBP. What arbitrage positions would create this rate of return?

#### Solution

The implied domestic repo rate can be found by rewriting the fair value relationship as

$$r_d = \left(\frac{F_0}{S_0}\right)^{1/t}\left(1 + r_f\right) - 1 = \left(\frac{1.630}{1.620}\right)^{10}\left(1 + 0.026\right) - 1$$

$$= 9.1\%.$$

To capture this return, the investor must convert dollars to pounds at the current exchange rate of USD1.620/GBP, invest at the foreign interest rate of 2.6%, and sell the futures contract. When the principal and interest in pounds are converted back into dollars and combined with the gains or losses on the futures contract, the realized dollar return on the strategy is 9.1% annualized minus any transaction costs.

## Basis and Calendar Spreads

### Exercise 4

Suppose that on 1 August, the S&P 500 is at 1,345.3, with September and December futures prices as shown in the following table. Two weeks later, on 15 August, the S&P 500 has fallen to 1,303.6, with the futures prices as shown in the following table.

|  | 1 August | 15 August |
|---|---|---|
| Index | 1,345.3 | 1,303.6 |
| September settlement | 1,342.6 | 1,301.8 |
| December settlement | 1,337.2 | 1,296.5 |

a. Calculate the nearby (September) futures contract basis at each of the two dates.

b. Calculate the calendar spread between the nearby (September) and deferred (December) futures for each of the two August dates.

### Solutions

a. The basis for the September S&P 500 futures is the spot minus the futures price. So, the basis on 1 August is $1,345.3 - 1,342.6 = 2.7$, and the basis on 15 August is $1,303.6 - 1,301.8 = 1.8$. As is typical, the basis declines as the contract settlement date approaches.

b. The calendar spread of 1 August is $1,342.6 - 1,337.2 = 5.4$, and the calendar spread on 15 August is $1,301.8 - 1,296.5 = 5.3$. As is typical, the calendar spread remains fairly constant over time.

## Hedging Relationships

### Exercise 5

Suppose an investor will receive a payment of 625 million yen in one month as a Japanese bond position matures. The current exchange rate is USD0.0125/JPY (or 80.0 yen per dollar), but the investor is concerned that the yen will depreciate relative to the dollar over the next month.

a.  Construct a simple hedge using the yen futures contracts, currently priced at USD0.0127/JPY. How many contracts would be needed?

b.  If the spot exchange rate decreases to 0.0121 over the next month and the futures price decreases to 0.0124, what is the net result of the hedge for the investor?

## Solutions

a.  The notional value of the yen futures contract is 12,500 (see Table 1.1), so to hedge a decline in the value of the yen (i.e., an increase in the JPY/USD exchange rate), the investor would need to take a short position in 625,000,000/12,500,000 = 50 futures contracts.

b.  The value of the 625 million yen at the final exchange rate of 0.0121 is 625,000,000 × 0.0121 = $7,562,500. The gain on the short futures position of 50 contracts is 50 × 12,500,000 × (0.0127 − 0.0124) = $187,500, for a total hedged value of 7,562,500 + 187,500 = $7,750,000. Note that the total hedged value is still $62,500 less than the value of the bond if it could have been immediately converted to dollars, 0.0125 × 625,000,000 = $7,812,500. The reason is that the hedge is subject to basis risk and the basis in the futures contract increased from 0.0127 − 0.0125 = 0.0002 to 0.0124 − 0.0121 = 0.0003.

## Exercise 6

Using the following cash and futures prices, calculate the effect of a Eurodollar hedge constructed using a stack compared with one using a strip. What net advantage has been created by using the strip?

|  | Now | Roll Date (t) | Hedge Date (T) |
|---|---|---|---|
| Spot price, $S$ | 98.85 | 97.55 | 97.50 |
| Nearby contract, $F^1$ | 97.50 | 97.45 | — |
| Deferred contract, $F^2$ | 97.25 | 97.25 | 97.20 |

## Solution

The net price of the hedge created using a strip is

$$P_T(\text{Strip}) = S_T + \left(F_0^2 - F_T^2\right) = 97.50 + (97.25 - 97.20) = 97.55.$$

The net price of the hedge created using a stack would be

$$P_T(\text{Stack}) = S_T + \left(F_0^1 - F_t^1\right) - \left(F_t^2 - F_T^2\right)$$
$$= 97.50 + (97.50 - 97.45) + (97.25 - 97.20)$$
$$= 97.60.$$

The difference between the net price of the stack and strip is caused by the change in the calendar spread from the initiation of the hedge (Time 0) to the point of the roll (time $t$):

$$P_T(\text{Stack}) - P_T(\text{Strip}) = \left(F_0^1 - F_0^2\right) - \left(F_t^1 - F_t^2\right)$$
$$= (97.50 - 97.25) - (97.45 - 97.25)$$
$$= 0.05.$$

## Interest Rate Concepts

### Exercise 7

Currently, the term structure (effective annual rates on zero-coupon bonds) is as follows.

| Maturity (years) | Effective Annual Rate |
|---|---|
| 1 | $y_1 = 2.05$ |
| 2 | $y_2 = 2.23$ |
| 3 | $y_3 = 2.41$ |

a.  Calculate the one-year implied forward rates for one and two years from now.

b.  Calculate the annualized two-year implied forward rate for one year from now.

### Solutions

a.  The one-year rate one year forward is

$$f_2 = \frac{(1+y_2)^2}{(1+y_1)^1} - 1 = \frac{(1.0223)^2}{(1.0205)^1} - 1 = 2.41\%,$$

and the one-year rate two years forward is

$$f_3 = \frac{(1+y_3)^3}{(1+y_2)^2} - 1 = \frac{(1.0241)^3}{(1.0223)^2} - 1 = 2.77\%.$$

b. The annualized two-year rate one year forward is

$$\left[(1+f_2)(1+f_3)\right]^{1/2} -1 = \left[(1.0241)\,(1.0277)\right]^{1/2} -1$$
$$= 2.59\%.$$

## Exercise 8

Consider an annual coupon bond with a face value of 100, exactly three years to maturity, and a 5.00% coupon. It is priced to yield 1.95%.

a. Calculate the price of the bond.

b. Calculate the bond's modified duration.

c. Calculate the bond's DV01, defined as the change in dollar value associated with a 1 bp change in yield.

d. Use the bond's modified duration to estimate the price impact of a 100 bps rise in yield to 2.95%.

e. Calculate the bond's modified convexity.

f. Use the bond's modified duration *and* modified convexity to estimate the price impact of a 100 bp rise in yield to 2.95%.

g. Calculate the *actual* price of the bond at a yield of 2.95% and contrast your answer to the estimates in Exercises 8d and 8f.

## Solutions

a. The sum of present values of the cash flows is

$$\frac{5}{(1.0195)^1} + \frac{5}{(1.0195)^2} + \frac{105}{(1.0195)^3} = 108.80.$$

The bond price relative to face value can also be calculated by the formula

$$p = \frac{c}{y}\left[1 - \frac{1}{(1+y)^T}\right] + \frac{1}{(1+y)^T}$$

$$= \frac{5.00}{1.95}\left[1 - \frac{1}{(1.0195)^3}\right] + \frac{100}{(1.0195)^3}$$

$$= 1.0880,$$

giving a price of $108.80.

b. Duration is the weighted average time to maturity of the bond's cash flows:

$$\frac{5}{(1.0195)^1}(1) + \frac{5}{(1.0195)^2}(2) + \frac{105}{(1.0195)^3}(3) = 2.866,$$

so the modified duration is 2.866/1.0195 = 2.81 years.

Modified duration can also be calculated by the formula

$$D^* = \frac{1}{y} - \frac{1+T(c-y)/(1+y)}{c\left[(1+y)^T - 1\right]+y}$$

$$= \frac{1}{0.0195} - \frac{1+3\left[(0.0500-0.0195)/1.0195\right]}{0.0500\left[(1.0195)^3 - 1\right]+0.0195}$$

$$= 2.81.$$

c.  The DV01 of the bond is

$$DV01 = D_B^* P_B(0.0001) = 2.81(108.80)(0.0001) = 0.0306.$$

d.  Using modified duration, a 100 bp increase in yield gives a drop in price of −2.81(0.0100) = −281 bps, or −2.81%.

e.  The convexity of the bond is

$$\frac{5}{(1.0195)^1}(1)(2)+\frac{5}{(1.0195)^2}(2)(3)+\frac{105}{(1.0195)^3}(3)(4)=11.284,$$

so the modified convexity is $11.284/(1.0195)^2 = 10.86$.

f.  Using modified convexity and modified duration, a 100 bp increase in yield gives a drop in price of −2.81(0.0100) + [10.86(0.0100)²]/2 = −276 bps, or −2.76%.

g.  The actual price at a yield of 2.95% is

$$\frac{5}{(1.0295)^1}+\frac{5}{(1.0295)^2}+\frac{105}{(1.0295)^3}=105.80,$$

which is a 105.80/108.80 − 1 = −2.76% drop in price. The estimated price impact of −2.81% found when using modified duration is an approximation. The refined estimate of −2.76% found when using both modified duration and modified convexity is more accurate.

## Hedge Positions

### Exercise 9

Calculate the hedge ratio and the number of futures contracts required for a short-term hedge of each of the following positions. Assume that all futures contracts in this problem expire in three months ($t = 0.25$ years) and that the effective annualized repo (risk-free) rate embedded in these contracts is 2.00%.

a.  Hedge a $50 million equity portfolio that has a beta of 0.9 relative to the S&P 500. The S&P 500 is currently at 1,350 and has a dividend yield of exactly 3.00%.

b.  How would the solution in Exercise 9a change if the hedge horizon was longer and equal to the three-month expiration of the equity index futures contract?

c.  Hedge a $50 million portfolio of corporate bonds using T-bond futures. Assume that corporate yields will change by 12 bps when T-bond rates change by 10 bps. The modified duration for the corporate bond portfolio is 6.3 years, and the modified duration for the T-bond futures is 8.7 years. The average price of the corporate bonds is 94 12/32; the futures is priced at 96 16/32; and the price of the CTD T-bond is 98 24/32.

d.  Hedge a £40 million exposure when the annualized risk-free three-month U.K. interest rate is 1.00%.

## Solutions

a.  The hedge ratio for the equity portfolio with a short hedge horizon is

$$h = \frac{-\beta}{(1+r-d)^t} = \frac{-0.9}{(1+0.0200-0.0300)^{0.25}} = -0.902.$$

The notional value per contract is 50 × 1,350 = $67,500, so the rounded number of contracts required is

$$n = h\left(\frac{\text{Value hedged}}{\text{Contract size}}\right) = -0.902\left(\frac{50,000,000}{67,500}\right) = -668,$$

meaning a short position in 668 S&P 500 futures contracts.

b.  If the hedge is expected to be in place until the expiration of the futures contract, the impact of the hedge will reflect the convergence of the futures contract to the index. The hedge ratio would not need to be adjusted for the current basis because the portfolio beta is 0.9. The number of futures contracts would be

$$n = h\left(\frac{\text{Value hedged}}{\text{Contract size}}\right) = -0.9\left(\frac{50,000,000}{67,500}\right) = -667.$$

A larger number of contracts (668 compared with 667) is required when the hedge is held for only a short time because little basis convergence will occur and a change in the futures index will produce a slightly smaller change in the futures price as a result of the currently negative basis. Consequently, a slightly larger number of contracts is needed for the hedge. The adjustment is not particularly meaningful, however, in this case.

c.  A cross-hedge can be constructed for the corporate bond portfolio with T-bond futures because changes in corporate and Treasury interest rates are assumed to be highly correlated. The hedge ratio for the portfolio is

$$h = -\frac{D_B^*}{D_F^*}\left(\frac{F}{B}\right)\left(\frac{\Delta y_B}{\Delta y_F}\right)$$

$$= -\frac{6.3}{8.7}\left(\frac{96.500}{94.375}\right)\left(\frac{12}{10}\right)$$

$$= -0.889.$$

The price of the CTD bond is 98.750, so the notional value of each futures contract is $0.98750 \times \$100,000 = \$98,750$. The number of short contracts required is

$$n = h\left(\frac{\text{Value hedged}}{\text{Contract size}}\right)$$

$$= -0.889\left(\frac{50,000,000}{98,750}\right)$$

$$= -450.$$

d.  The hedge ratio for the British pound exposure is

$$h = -\left(\frac{1+r_f}{1+r_d}\right)^t = -\left(\frac{1.0100}{1.0200}\right)^{0.25} = -0.998.$$

Given that the U.S. and U.K. interest rates are similar, the hedge ratio is quite close to –1.0 and is often simply assumed to be exactly –1.000 in practice. Given the calculated hedge ratio of –0.998, however, and a contract size of £62,500, the number of contracts required is

$$n = h\left(\frac{\text{Value hedged}}{\text{Contract size}}\right)$$

$$= -0.998\left(\frac{40,000,000}{62,500}\right)$$

$$= -639.$$

## Exercise 10

Suppose an investor has a multi-asset portfolio consisting of the $50 million stock portfolio in Exercise 9a, the $50 million bond portfolio in Exercise 9c, and \$25 million in cash—that is, weights of $w_S = 50/125 = 40\%$, $w_B = 50/125 = 40\%$, and $100 - 40 - 40 = 20\%$ in cash. The investor would like a portfolio that has the characteristics of a 60/30/10 stock/bond/cash portfolio, in which the target equity portfolio has a standard beta of 1.0 and the target bond portfolio has a duration of exactly 10.0 years. Without changing the actual physical assets in the portfolio, how many futures contracts of what type are needed to achieve the target portfolio weights and risk exposures?

## Solution

The hedge ratio for the desired equity exposure is

$$h_S = \frac{w_S^T - w_S \beta_S}{(1+r-d)^t}$$

$$= \frac{(0.60-0.40)0.900}{(1+0.0200-0.0300)^{0.25}}$$

$$= 0.241,$$

meaning that a long equity futures hedge is required to increase the equity exposure and the equity beta. Specifically, the required number of S&P 500 futures contracts is

$$n = h\left(\frac{\text{Value hedged}}{\text{Contract size}}\right)$$

$$= 0.241\left(\frac{50,000,000}{67,500}\right)$$

$$= 179.$$

The hedge ratio for the desired bond exposure is

$$h_B = \left(\frac{w_B^T D_T^* - w_B D_B^*}{D_F^*}\right)\left(\frac{B}{F}\right)\left(\frac{\Delta y_B}{\Delta y_F}\right)$$

$$= \left(\frac{0.30(10.0-0.40)6.3}{8.7}\right)\left(\frac{94.375}{96.500}\right)\left(\frac{12}{10}\right)$$

$$= 0.065.$$

Even though the target weight of 30% is lower than the actual weight of 40%, the desired duration of 10.0 is enough higher than the actual duration of 6.3 that a long bond futures position is needed. The number of contracts required is

$$n = h\left(\frac{\text{Value hedged}}{\text{Contract size}}\right) = 0.065\left(\frac{50,000,000}{98,750}\right) = 33.$$

# Risk–Return Characteristics of Options

## Exercise 11

This exercise considers several strategies in addition to those discussed in Chapter 4 to illustrate the payoff patterns of options and some intuition about their relative prices. The options in each strategy are for the same expiration date, but none of the underlying security is held, so these strategies are spreads and generally considered to be somewhat speculative, in contrast to hedges. Prepare a contingency table and payoff diagram, including a dotted line for the payoff net of the initial cash flow, for each of the following:

a. *Short straddle.* Sell a put and sell a call with the same strike price, $X$.

b. *Bear put spread.* Sell a put with a strike price of $X_1$ and buy a put at a strike price of $X_2$ (where $X_1 < X_2$).

c. *Ratio spread.* Buy a call option at a strike price of $X_1$ and sell two call options with a strike price of $X_2$ (where $X_1 < X_2$).

d. *Butterfly spread.* Buy two different call options at strike prices $X_1$ and $X_3$ and sell two call options at strike price $X_2$ (where $X_1 < X_2 < X_3$). For this problem, assume that $X_2$ is halfway between $X_1$ and $X_3$.

e. *Condor.* Sell two different call options at strike prices $X_2$ and $X_3$ and buy two different call options at strike prices $X_1$ and $X_4$ (where $X_1 < X_2 < X_3 < X_4$). For this problem, assume that the difference between the two lower strike prices, $X_2 - X_1$, is equal to the difference between the two higher strike prices, $X_4 - X_3$.

f. *Box spread.* Buy a call option with strike price $X_1$ and sell a call option with strike price $X_2$. In addition, sell a put option at strike price $X_1$ and buy a put option at strike price $X_2$ (where $X_1 < X_2$).

## Solutions

a. The short straddle is constructed by selling a put and a call option with the same strike price. The contingency table for the short straddle follows.

| | $S_T < X$ | $S_T > X$ |
|---|---|---|
| – Call option | 0 | $-(S_T - X)$ |
| – Put option | $-(X - S_T)$ | 0 |
| Total payoff | $S_T - X$ | $X - S_T$ |

The payoff structure of the short straddle is shown in **Figure E.1**, with a dotted line for the payoff "net" of the purchase prices of the call and put options. Because both options are sold in this strategy, the initial cash flow is positive and the dotted line is plotted above the solid line. The short straddle yields a positive net profit as long as the security stays close to the strike price. If the security moves away from the strike price in either direction by more than the combined option premiums, the short straddle shows a loss. The motivation for this speculative strategy is a belief that the realized volatility of the underlying security will not be as high as the volatility implied by the option prices.

**Figure E.1. Payoff Profile of a Short Straddle**

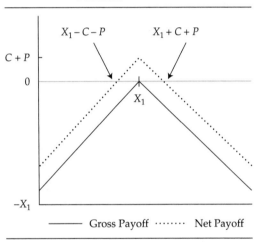

b. The bear put spread is constructed by buying a put option at a high strike price, $X_2$, and selling a put option at a lower strike price, $X_1$. The contingency table follows.

|  | $S_T < X_1$ | $X_1 < S_T < X_2$ | $S_T > X_2$ |
|---|---|---|---|
| Put option at $X_2$ | $X_2 - S_T$ | $X_2 - S_T$ | 0 |
| – Put option at $X_1$ | $-(X_1 - S_T)$ | 0 | 0 |
| Total payoff | $X_2 - X_1$ | $X_2 - S_T$ | 0 |

The payoff profile of the bear put spread is shown in **Figure E.2**. The bear put spread yields a positive net payoff if the security price drops below the breakeven point, which is the higher strike price, $X_2$, minus the cost of establishing the spread. The cost of the spread is equal to the price paid for the higher strike-price put, $P_2$, minus the price received for the lower strike-price put, $P_1$. By arbitrage, we know that $P_2 > P_1$, so the cost is positive. In addition, we know that $P_2 - P_1 < X_2 - X_1$. Otherwise, the dotted line would fall entirely below zero, which would create an arbitrage opportunity for someone by reversing the positions and generating a riskless return with no investment. The motivation for this strategy is a bearish outlook for the security with limited potential gains and losses.

**Figure E.2.    Payoff Profile of a Bear Put Spread**

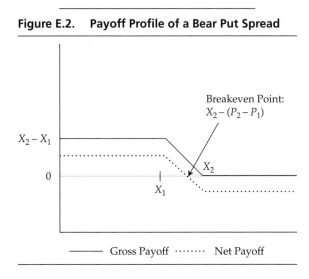

c.   The *ratio spread* or *upside ratio spread* is constructed by buying a call option at a low strike price and selling two call options at a higher strike price. The contingency table follows.

|  | $S_T < X_1$ | $X_1 < S_T < X_2$ | $S_T > X_2$ |
|---|---|---|---|
| Call option at $X_1$ | 0 | $S_T - X_1$ | $S_T - X_1$ |
| – Two call options at $X_2$ | 0 | 0 | $-2(S_T - X_2)$ |
| Total payoff | 0 | $S_T - X_1$ | $2X_2 - X_1 - S_T$ |

The payoff profile of the ratio spread is shown in **Figure E.3**. The net profit is positive as long as the security price remains below the breakeven point, which is above the higher strike price, although the largest net profit is around the higher strike price. Beyond the breakeven point, the spread loses $2.00 for every $1.00 increase in the security price; in other words, the right-most part of the payoff profile is steeper (2 for 1 instead of 1 for 1) than it is for many other option strategies. A "downside" ratio spread is constructed by buying one put option and selling two others at a lower strike price.

**Figure E.3.  Payoff Profile of a Ratio Spread**

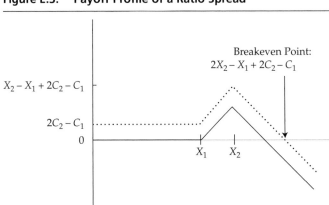

———— Gross Payoff    ········ Net Payoff

d.  A butterfly spread is constructed by buying two call options with separate strike prices and selling two call options with a strike price between the long call options. The contingency table follows.

|  | $S_T < X_1$ | $X_1 < S_T < X_2$ | $X_2 < S_T < X_3$ | $S_T > X_3$ |
|---|---|---|---|---|
| Call option at $X_1$ | 0 | $S_T - X_1$ | $S_T - X_1$ | $S_T - X_1$ |
| Call option at $X_3$ | 0 | 0 | 0 | $S_T - X_3$ |
| – Two call options at $X_2$ | 0 | 0 | $-2(S_T - X_2)$ | $-2(S_T - X_2)$ |
| Total payoff | 0 | $S_T - X_1$ | $2X_2 - X_1 - S_T$ | $2X_2 - X_1 - X_3$ |

The payoff profile for the butterfly spread is shown in **Figure E.4**. Because the strike prices are equally spaced in this example, the gross payoff profile for high and low prices of the stock is zero. The dotted line (net payoff) must lie below the solid line (i.e., the cost of the options purchased exceeds the cost of the options sold) or there would be an arbitrage opportunity. Similar to the short straddle, the motivation for the butterfly spread is the belief that the underlying security is going to have lower realized volatility than the volatility implied by the option prices. In contrast to the short straddle, the downside risk of the butterfly spread is limited. This strategy results in negative net profits as the security price moves beyond the outside strike prices.

**Figure E.4. Payoff Profile of a Butterfly Spread**

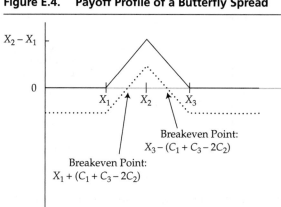

——— Gross Payoff   ········· Net Payoff

e. A condor is constructed by selling two call options with separate strike prices near the money and buying two additional call options with strike prices outside the two short positions. The condor is similar to the butterfly spread except that the two short positions have different strike prices. The contingency table follows.

| | $S_T < X_1$ | $X_1 < S_T < X_2$ | $X_2 < S_T < X_3$ | $X_3 < S_T < X_4$ | $S_T > X_4$ |
|---|---|---|---|---|---|
| Call option at $X_1$ | 0 | $S_T - X_1$ | $S_T - X_1$ | $S_T - X_1$ | $S_T - X_1$ |
| – Call option at $X_2$ | 0 | 0 | $-(S_T - X_2)$ | $-(S_T - X_2)$ | $-(S_T - X_2)$ |
| – Call option at $X_3$ | 0 | 0 | 0 | $-(S_T - X_3)$ | $-(S_T - X_3)$ |
| Call option at $X_4$ | 0 | 0 | 0 | 0 | $S_T - X_4$ |
| Total payoff | 0 | $S_T - X_1$ | $X_2 - X_1$ | $\begin{array}{c} X_3 + X_2 \\ -S_T - X_1 \end{array}$ | $\begin{array}{c} X_3 + X_2 \\ -X_4 - X_1 = 0 \end{array}$ |

The payoff profile for the condor is shown in **Figure E.5**. If the outside pairs of strike prices are equally spaced, the gross payoff profile for high and low prices of the stock is zero. The dotted line (net payoff) must lie below the solid line (the cost of the options purchased exceeds the cost of the options sold) or there would be an arbitrage opportunity. Similar to

**Figure E.5.  Payoff Profile of a Condor**

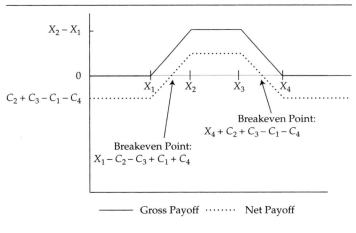

——— Gross Payoff  ·········· Net Payoff

the short straddle and butterfly spread, the motivation for the condor is the belief that the underlying security is going to have less realized volatility than the volatility implied by the option prices.

f.  The box spread is really a spread of two spreads—constructed by buying a bull call spread and selling a bull put spread. The pair of option strike prices for the put and call spreads are the same, with $X_2$ greater than $X_1$. The box spread can also be thought of as two put–call parity pairs, one long and the other short. The contingency table follows.

|  | $S_T < X_1$ | $X_1 < S_T < X_2$ | $S_T > X_2$ |
|---|---|---|---|
| Call option at $X_1$ | 0 | $S_T - X_1$ | $S_T - X_1$ |
| – Call option at $X_2$ | 0 | 0 | $-(S_T - X_2)$ |
| – Put option at $X_1$ | $-(X_1 - S_T)$ | 0 | 0 |
| Put option at $X_2$ | $X_2 - S_T$ | $X_2 - S_T$ | 0 |
| Total payoff | $X_2 - X_1$ | $X_2 - X_1$ | $X_2 - X_1$ |

The payoff profile for the box spread, shown in **Figure E.6**, is a constant, $X_2 - X_1$, the same no matter what happens to the security price. Because the payoff is constant, the four options should be priced to give a net payoff equal to the riskless interest rate by arbitrage. In fact, the cost of the box spread, which is $(C_1 + P_2) - (C_2 + P_1)$, is equal to the present value of the difference in strike prices at the riskless rate: $(X_2 - X_1)/(1 + r)^T$.

## Figure E.6.   Payoff Profile of a Box Spread

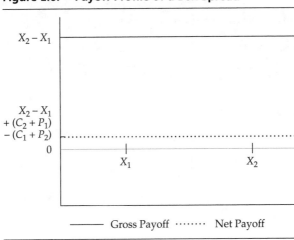

$X_2 - X_1$

$X_2 - X_1$
$+ (C_2 + P_1)$
$- (C_1 + P_2)$
0

$X_1$          $X_2$

——— Gross Payoff   ········ Net Payoff

# Option Pricing

### Exercise 12

Consider a non-dividend-paying stock currently priced at $S_0$ = $100. In the binomial pricing approach, the stock will either move up to a price of $S_u$ = $115 or move down to a price of $S_d$ = $90 at time $T$ (e.g., $T$ = 1.0). Consider a call and put option with a strike price of $X$ = $95. In this exercise, in order to focus on arbitrage pricing and hedging relationships, we will assume a risk-free interest rate of exactly zero (i.e., 0.00%) over time $T$.

a.  Calculate the fair (i.e., arbitrage-free) price of the call option.

b.  Calculate the fair (i.e., arbitrage-free) price of the put option.

c.  Using only the stock and a risk-free bond, create the same payoff as the call option.

d.  Although not stated previously, assume the actual probabilities of the stock going up to $S_u$ = $115 or down to $S_d$ = $95 are, respectively, 60% and 40%, so the expected price of the stock is 0.60(115) + 0.40(90) = $105, giving an expected return 5.0%. How would the fair price of the call option change if the actual probabilities of the stock moving up or down were 80% and 20% (i.e., an expected return of 10.0%)?

e.  Suppose the spread of terminal stock prices was wider, at $S_u$ = $130 and $S_d$ = $80 (instead of $S_u$ = $115 and $S_d$ = $90). How would this change affect the fair price of the call option?

### Solutions

a. The call option payoff if the stock goes up is

$$C_u = \max(S_u - X, 0)$$
$$= \max(115 - 95, 0)$$
$$= \$20,$$

and if the stock goes down,

$$C_d = \max(S_d - X, 0)$$
$$= \max(90 - 95, 0)$$
$$= \$0.$$

The hedge ratio for the call option is

$$h_C = \frac{C_u - C_d}{S_u - S_d}$$
$$= \frac{20 - 0}{115 - 90}$$
$$= 0.80,$$

meaning that owning 0.80 shares of the stock will offset the risk of writing (i.e., selling) the call option. Specifically, a portfolio that is long 0.80 shares and short the call option will have a payoff of $0.80(115) - 20 = 0.80(90) - 0 = \$72$ no matter which way the stock goes. Given that the terminal value is certain, the upfront cost of the portfolio, $0.25(50) - C_0$, must be equal to the present value of $72, which with the zero interest rate assumption is just $72. Solving for the cost of the call option in this arbitrage-based equality, $0.80(100) - C_0 = 72$, gives $C_0 = \$8.00$. However, this calculation can be done more directly with the "risk-neutral" probability value,

$$q = \frac{S_0(1+r)^T - S_d}{S_u - S_d}$$
$$= \frac{100(1) - 90}{115 - 90}$$
$$= 0.40,$$

and the call option pricing formula,

$$C_0 = \frac{qC_u + (1-q)C_d}{(1+r)^T}$$
$$= \frac{0.40(20) + 0.60(0)}{1}$$
$$= 8.00.$$

Note that the expected stock price when the risk-neutral probabilities are used is 0.40(115) + 0.60(90) = 100, so the expected return with these risk-neutral probabilities is zero, the risk-free rate in this exercise.

b. The put option payoff if the stock goes up is

$$P_u = \max(X - S_u, 0)$$
$$= \max(95 - 115, 0)$$
$$= \$0,$$

and if the stock goes down,

$$P_d = \max(X - S_d, 0)$$
$$= \max(95 - 90, 0)$$
$$= \$5.$$

The hedge ratio for the put option is

$$h_P = \frac{P_u - P_d}{S_u - S_d}$$
$$= \frac{0 - 5}{115 - 90}$$
$$= -0.20,$$

which is the binomial model equivalent to the Black–Scholes delta (i.e., the delta of the call option was 0.80). Because of put–call parity, the delta of the put is equal to the delta of the call option minus 1.0. Using the risk-neutral probabilities, we find the price of the put option to be

$$P_0 = \frac{qP_u + (1-q)P_d}{(1+r)^T}$$
$$= \frac{0.40(0) + 0.60(5)}{(1)}$$
$$= 3.00.$$

The put price can also be verified, given the calculated call price, by the put–call parity relationship:

$$P_0 = C_0 - S_0 + \frac{X}{(1+r)^T}$$
$$= 8 - 100 + \frac{95}{1}$$
$$= 3.00.$$

c. The call option payoff of 20 or 0 can be replicated by borrowing $72 to purchase $h_C = 0.80$ shares at $100 per share. After paying off the $72 loan (at zero interest), the total payoff will be $0.80(115) - 72 = 20$ if the stock goes up and $0.80(90) - 72 = 0$ if the stock goes down.

d. The actual probabilities of the stock going up or down were never part of the arbitrage-free pricing argument; only the hypothetical risk-neutral probabilities were used. So, a change in the expected return, with the current price of $S_0 = \$100$ held fixed, does not affect the price of the options.

e. The call option payoff if the stock goes up is now

$$C_u = \max\left(S_u - X, 0\right)$$
$$= \max\left(130 - 95, 0\right)$$
$$= \$35,$$

but if the stock goes down,

$$C_d = \max\left(S_d - X, 0\right)$$
$$= \max\left(80 - 95, 0\right)$$
$$= \$0.$$

The hedge ratio for the call option is now

$$h_C = \frac{C_u - C_d}{S_u - S_d}$$
$$= \frac{35 - 0}{130 - 80}$$
$$= 0.70,$$

meaning that owning 0.70 shares of the stock will offset the risk of writing (i.e., selling) the call option. The risk-neutral probability value is

$$q = \frac{S_0(1+r)^T - S_d}{S_u - S_d}$$
$$= \frac{100(1) - 80}{130 - 80}$$
$$= 0.40,$$

and the call option pricing formula gives

$$C_0 = \frac{qC_u + (1-q)C_d}{(1+r)^T}$$
$$= \frac{0.60(35) + 0.60(0)}{(1)}$$
$$= 14.00,$$

which is higher than the previous price of 8.00 because of the higher volatility (wider spread in stock prices) in the underlying security. Note that using the put–call parity relationship gives the put price as

$$P_0 = C_0 - S_0 + \frac{X}{(1+r)^T} = 14.00 - 100 + \frac{95}{1} = 9.00,$$

which is also higher than the previous price of 3.00 because of the increased volatility in the underlying security.

## Exercise 13

Consider options on a non-dividend-paying stock and the following Black–Scholes parameters: $S_0$ = \$82.40, $X$ = \$85.00, $T$ = 0.25 (three months), $r$ = 2.00%, and $\sigma$ = 34%.

a.  Calculate the fair price of a European call option using the Black–Scholes formula.

b.  Calculate the fair price for a European put option using the Black–Scholes formula.

c.  Calculate the price of the call option with one week ($T$ = 0.02), instead of three months, to expiration if the stock price is still $S_0$ = \$82.40 and none of the other parameters have changed.

d.  Returning to the options with three months to expiration, approximately how low would the stock price have to be for possible early exercise of an American put option?

e.  Suppose the quoted market price of the European call and put options in Exercises 13a and 13b of this problem are, respectively, $c_0$ = \$5.50 and $p_0$ = \$7.50. Using an analytic formula, what is the volatility implied by these prices? What is the exact implied volatility of the quoted call price when the Black–Scholes formula is used?

## Solutions

a.  Referring to the cumulative normal probability values gives

$$N(d_1) = N\left[ \frac{\ln(82.40/85.00) + (0.02 + 0.34^2/2)(0.25)}{0.34\sqrt{0.25}} \right]$$
$$= N(-0.06833)$$
$$= 0.473$$

and

$$N(d_2) = N\left[\frac{\ln(82.40/85.00) + (0.02 - 0.34^2/2)(0.25)}{0.34\sqrt{0.25}}\right]$$

$$= N(-0.23833)$$

$$= 0.406.$$

The current price of the call option is, thus,

$$c_0 = 82.40(0.473) - 85.00e^{-0.02(0.25)}(0.406)$$

$$= \$4.63.$$

b. The price of the corresponding put option is

$$p_0 = -82.40(1 - 0.473) + 85.00e^{-0.02(0.25)}(1 - 0.406)$$

$$= \$6.81.$$

c. Referring to the cumulative normal probability values gives

$$N(d_1) = N\left[\frac{\ln(82.40/85.00) + (0.02 + 0.34^2/2)(0.02)}{0.34\sqrt{0.02}}\right]$$

$$= N(-0.61372)$$

$$= 0.270$$

and

$$N(d_2) = N\left[\frac{\ln(82.40/85.00) + (0.02 - 0.34^2/2)(0.02)}{0.34\sqrt{0.02}}\right]$$

$$= N(-0.66181)$$

$$= 0.254.$$

The current price of the call option is, thus,

$$c_0 = 82.40(0.270) - 85.00\,e^{-0.02(0.02)}(0.254)$$

$$= \$0.64,$$

which is quite low because the option is one week from expiring out of the money.

d. The exercise value of the put option in Exercise 13b is $85.00 - 82.40 =$ $2.60, well below the fair market price of $6.81. Recalculating the Black–Scholes formula with the underlying stock price at $65 per share, however, gives a European put value of $19.91, below the exercise value at that stock price of $85.00 - 65.00 = $20.00. So, early exercise at that price or lower might be preferred. Of course, if the put were American, early exercise would have been anticipated by the market and built into the price. For example, a numerical routine (not provided in this tutorial) gives a fair American put price of $20.11 at the underlying stock price of $65, so early exercise would not quite be preferred. According to the numerical American put-pricing routine, the underlying stock price would have to fall to about $61 or lower to be exercised early.

e. The approximate volatility implied by the quoted option prices is

$$\sigma = \frac{C_0 + P_0}{2S_0} \sqrt{\frac{2\pi}{T}}$$

$$= \frac{5.50 + 7.50}{2(82.40)} \sqrt{\frac{2\pi}{0.25}}$$

$$= 39.5,$$

which is higher than the assumed 34.0% volatility in this problem because the quoted option prices are higher than the fair values calculated in Exercises 13a and 13b. The exact implied volatility for the call option based on the Black–Scholes formula (i.e., the volatility parameter that results in a $5.50 call price) is 39.3%.

## Exercise 14

Suppose a stock follows a two-period binomial process as shown in **Figure E.7**. The stock price starts at $100 and can increase by $10 or fall by $5 each period. At the end of the first period, the stock pays a dividend of $4 and the ex-dividend price drops by that amount. Notice that the price movements are absolute, not proportional, so the arbitrage-based hedge will change over time as the stock price moves. Consider a call option with a strike price of $100 (currently at the money) and an interest rate of 3.00% per period.

a. Calculate the price of a European call option.

b. Incorporating the ex-dividend prices, calculate the price of an American call option that can be exercised at Time 1, just before the dividend is paid.

## Solution

a. Finding the value for the call option requires finding the price of the option at each stage by working backward from Time 2 to Time 1 to Time 0. At Time 2, a call option with a strike price of $100 will have a value of $16.00 or $1.00 or will expire out of the money with a value of zero. If the stock price rises in the first period, the ex-dividend value of the call option is given by using Equations 5.21 and 5.22:

$$q_u = \frac{S_u(1+r) - S_{ud}}{S_{uu} - S_{ud}} = \frac{106(1.03) - 101}{116 - 101} = 0.545$$

and

$$C_u = \frac{q_u C_{uu} + (1 - q_u) C_{ud}}{(1+r)}$$

$$= \frac{(0.545)16 + (1 - 0.545)1}{(1.03)}$$

$$= 8.91.$$

If the stock price falls in the first period, the value of the ex-dividend call option is given by

$$q_d = \frac{S_d(1+r) - S_{dd}}{S_{du} - S_{dd}} = \frac{91(1.03) - 86}{101 - 86} = 0.515$$

and

$$C_d = \frac{q_d C_{du} + (1 - q_d) C_{dd}}{(1+r)}$$

$$= \frac{(0.515)1 + (1 - 0.515)0}{(1.03)}$$

$$= 0.50.$$

**Figure E.7.  Two-Period Binomial Process**

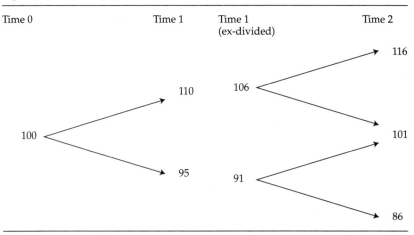

Based on these results at Time 1, the value of the European call option at Time 0 is given by

$$q = \frac{S_0(1+r)^T - S_d}{S_u - S_d}$$
$$= \frac{100(1.03) - 91}{106 - 91}$$
$$= 0.800$$

and

$$C_0 = \frac{qC_u + (1-q)C_d}{(1+r)^T}$$
$$= \frac{(0.800)8.91 + (1-0.800)0.50}{(1.03)}$$
$$= 7.02.$$

b. If the stock rises in the first period, the pre-dividend exercise value of the American call is 110 − 100 = $10, more than the value of $8.91 ex-dividend, so early exercise is optimal. If the stock price falls in the first period, the option is out of the money, so early exercise would be of no value, and in fact, it would be less than the $0.50 value ex-dividend. Because the hedge is based on the ex-dividend stock price, $q$ is still 0.800 for the American call option, but the Time 0 value of the American call is

$$C_0 = \frac{qC_u + (1-q)C_d}{(1+r)^T}$$
$$= \frac{(0.800)10.00 + (1-0.800)0.50}{(1.03)}$$
$$= 7.86.$$

Thus, the ability to exercise early adds 7.86 − 7.02 = $0.84 to the value of the American call option on this dividend-paying stock.

# Option Sensitivities and Hedging

### Exercise 15

Consider a put option with a delta of −0.289.

a. How many options per share would be required to create a delta-neutral hedge for the underlying stock?

b. Instead of a delta-neutral hedge, suppose an investor wanted the hedged stock to maintain a delta of 0.5. How many put options per share would then be required?

c. Consider a call option with the same strike price and maturity as the put option in this exercise. How many call options would be required to maintain a hedged delta of 0.5?

d. Using both the put and call option in this exercise, how would an investor create a delta-neutral and vega-neutral hedge on a share of the underlying stock?

### Solutions

a. The general hedging relationship given in Chapter 6 is

$$h = \frac{\Delta_V - \Delta_1}{\Delta_2},$$

where $\Delta_V$ is the desired hedge delta (i.e., zero for a delta-neutral hedge), $\Delta_1$ is the delta of the underlying security (1.0 by definition), and $\Delta_2$ is the delta of the option. So, in this case, the number of put options required per share is

$$h = \frac{\Delta_V - \Delta_1}{\Delta_2}$$
$$= \frac{0 - 1.0}{-0.289}$$
$$= 3.46.$$

b. If an investor wants to maintain a net delta of 0.5, the number of put options required is

$$h = \frac{\Delta_V - \Delta_1}{\Delta_2}$$
$$= \frac{0.5 - 1.0}{-0.289}$$
$$= 1.73.$$

c. The delta of the corresponding call option is $1 - 0.289 = 0.711$, so the number of call options required is

$$h = \frac{\Delta_V - \Delta_1}{\Delta_2}$$
$$= \frac{0.5 - 1.0}{0.711}$$
$$= -0.70,$$

meaning that one would *sell* 0.70 call options to produce a delta of the hedged stock position of 0.5.

d.   Delta and vega neutrality require that the following two equations be satisfied simultaneously:

$$\Delta_s + h_c\Delta_c + h_p\Delta_p = 0$$

and

$$v_s + h_c v_c + h_p v_p = 0.$$

The delta and vega of the underlying stock are 1 and 0 by definition. Although we don't know the vega for these options, we do know that they are positive and equal. We also know that the delta for the put is equal to the delta for the call minus 1. With all these conditions, the only possible solution to the two equations is to buy 1.0 put option and sell 1.0 call option. To see this conclusion, note that satisfying the vega-neutral condition requires that $h_c + h_p = 0$, resulting in the delta-neutral condition of $h_c = -1$. Other nonunity solutions would be possible only by using options with a *different* strike price for each option.

## Exercise 16

**Table E.1** gives sensitivity measures for various put and call options using the Black–Scholes model, with $S_0 = 100$ (other parameters are $T = 0.25$, $r = 1.00\%$, and $\sigma = 50\%$.)

Using the values in Table E.1, calculate the price and net sensitivity measures for each of the following strategies.

a.   *Short straddle.* Sell 100-strike call and 100-strike put.

b.   *Bear put spread.* Sell 90-strike put and buy 110-strike put.

c.   *Butterfly spread.* Buy 90-strike call and 110-strike call; sell two 100-strike calls.

**Table E.1.   Option Prices and Sensitivities**

|  | Price | Delta | Gamma | Theta | Rho | Vega |
|---|---|---|---|---|---|---|
| Call at $X = 90$ | 15.411 | 0.711 | 0.014 | −0.045 | 0.139 | 0.171 |
| Call at $X = 100$ | 10.061 | 0.554 | 0.016 | −0.053 | 0.113 | 0.198 |
| Call at $X = 110$ | 6.275 | 0.403 | 0.015 | −0.052 | 0.085 | 0.194 |
| Put at $X = 90$ | 5.186 | −0.289 | 0.014 | −0.043 | −0.085 | 0.171 |
| Put at $X = 100$ | 9.811 | −0.446 | 0.016 | −0.050 | −0.136 | 0.198 |
| Put at $X = 110$ | 16.000 | −0.597 | 0.015 | −0.049 | −0.189 | 0.194 |

d. *Box spread.* Buy 90-strike call, sell 110-strike call, sell 90-strike put, and buy 110-strike put.

## Solutions

The price and sensitivity measures for a combination of options can be calculated by summing the respective measures of each individual position, with a negative sign for options that are sold. For example, the net delta of the short straddle is −(0.554 − 0.446) = −0.108. The solutions for all parts of this exercise are shown in **Table E.2**.

Note that the short straddle has little sensitivity to changes in the underlying stock price, as measured by delta, but has a large negative sensitivity to changes in the volatility of the underlying stock, as measured by vega. The bear put spread, however, has a large negative delta but smaller vega. Like the short straddle, the butterfly has little delta—that is, it is directionally neutral—but has a negative vega with respect to the volatility of the stock. Because of their negative vegas, the short straddle and butterfly are sometimes referred to as *short volatility spreads*. The box spread is, by design, delta, gamma, and vega neutral, meaning that the spread price is insensitive to changes in underlying stock price or volatility. In fact, the price of the box spread in this example is simply the present value of 20, the difference in the strike prices of the constituent options. As a present value, the price of the box spread does have sensitivities to time to expiration, as measured by theta, and the risk-free interest rate, as measured by rho.

Table E.2.   **Option Spread Prices and Sensitivity Measures**

|  | Price | Delta | Gamma | Theta | Rho | Vega |
|---|---|---|---|---|---|---|
| Short straddle | −19.872 | −0.108 | −0.032 | 0.103 | 0.023 | −0.396 |
| Bear put spread | 10.814 | −0.308 | 0.001 | −0.006 | −0.104 | 0.023 |
| Butterfly spread | 1.564 | 0.006 | −0.003 | 0.009 | −0.002 | −0.031 |
| Box spread | 19.950 | 0.000 | 0.000 | 0.001 | −0.050 | 0.000 |

# Synthetic Option Positions

## Exercise 17

Using the put–call parity relationship, describe which combination of securities creates each position synthetically:

a. Call option.

b. Put option.

c. Riskless bond.

d. Covered call.

e. Protective put.

## Solutions

The basic European put–call parity for a non-dividend-paying stock is

$$c_o - p_0 = S_0 - \frac{X}{(1+r)^T},$$

which can be expressed in various ways to illustrate the creation of synthetic positions.

a. The synthetic call can be created by borrowing the present value of $X$ while purchasing the security plus a put option with the same maturity and exercise price:

$$c_o = p_0 + S_0 - \frac{X}{(1+r)^T}.$$

b. The put option would be the equivalent of

$$p_o = c_0 - S_0 + \frac{X}{(1+r)^T},$$

which indicates that shorting the security to purchase a call option of the same maturity and strike price with the rest invested in a riskless bond will mimic a put option.

c. The riskless bond would be the equivalent of

$$\frac{X}{(1+r)^T} = p_o - c_0 + S_0,$$

so purchasing a security plus a put option and selling a call option with the same maturity and strike price creates a synthetic bond.

d. A covered call would be the equivalent of

$$S_0 - c_o = \frac{X}{(1+r)^T} - p_0,$$

so selling a put option and investing in a riskless bond gives the same payoff as the covered call.

e.  A protective put would be the equivalent of

$$S_0 + p_o = \frac{X}{(1+r)^T} + c_0,$$

so purchasing a call and investing in a riskless bond gives the same payoff as the protective put. This alternative combination is sometimes referred to as a *90/10 strategy* because about 90% of the portfolio is invested in cash and 10% is spent on call options.

# References

## Current General References on Derivatives

Bodie, Zvi, Alex Kane, and Alan Marcus. 2011. *Investments*. 9th ed. New York: McGraw-Hill Irwin.

Hull, John C. 2012. *Options, Futures, and Other Derivatives*. 8th ed. Upper Saddle River, NJ: Prentice-Hall.

McDonald, Robert L. 2009. *Derivative Markets*. 3rd ed. London: Pearson.

## Academic Papers on Derivatives after 1990

Bakshi, G., C. Cao, and Z. Chen. 1997. "Empirical Performance of Alternative Option Pricing Models." *Journal of Finance*, vol. 52, no. 5 (December):2003–2049.

Brennan, M.J., and E.S. Schwartz. 1990. "Arbitrage in Stock Index Futures." *Journal of Business*, vol. 63, no. 1 (January):S7–S31.

Broadie, M., and J. Detemple. 1996. "American Option Valuation: New Bounds, Approximations, and Comparison of Existing Methods." *Review of Financial Studies*, vol. 9, no. 4 (October):1211–1250.

Brown, G.W. 2001. "Managing Foreign Exchange Risk with Derivatives." *Journal of Financial Econometrics*, vol. 60, nos. 2–3 (May):401–448.

Coval, J.D., and T. Shumway. 2001. "Expected Option Returns." *Journal of Finance*, vol. 56, no. 3 (June):983–1009.

Figlewski, S., and B. Gao. 1999. "The Adaptive Mesh Model: A New Approach to Efficient Option Pricing." *Journal of Financial Economics*, vol. 53, no. 3 (September):313–351.

Grinblatt, M., and N. Jegadeesh. 1996. "The Relative Price of Eurodollar Futures and Forward Contracts." *Journal of Finance*, vol. 51, no. 4 (September):1499–1522.

Heath, D., R. Jarrow, and A. Merton. 1992. "Bond Pricing and the Term-Structure of Interest Rates: A New Methodology for Contingent Claims Pricing." *Econometrica*, vol. 60, no. 1 (January):77–105.

Heston, S. 1993. "A Closed-Form Solution for Options with Stochastic Volatility with Applications to Bond and Currency Options." *Review of Financial Studies*, vol. 6, no. 2 (April):327–343.

Hull, J.C., and A. White. 1995. "The Impact of Default Risk on the Prices of Options and Other Derivative Securities." *Journal of Banking & Finance*, vol. 19, no. 2 (May):299–322.

Rubinstein, Mark. 1994. "Implied Binomial Trees." *Journal of Finance*, vol. 49, no. 3 (July):771–818.

## General References on Futures

Arak, Marcelle, Laurie Goodman, and Susan Ross. 1986. "The Cheapest to Deliver Bond on a Treasury Bond Futures Contract." In *Advances in Futures and Options Research*, 1, Part B. Edited by Frank Fabozzi. Oxford, United Kingdom: JAI Press.

Black, Fischer. 1976. "The Pricing of Commodity Contracts." *Journal of Financial Economics*, vol. 3, nos. 1–2 (January/February):167–179.

Bookstaber, Richard M. 1985. *The Complete Investment Book*. Glenview, IL: Scott Foresman Trade.

Chance, D. 1989. *An Introduction to Options and Futures*. Fort Worth, TX: Dryden Press.

Hull, J. 1989. *Options, Futures, and Other Derivative Securities*. Boston: Prentice-Hall.

Johnson, L.L. 1960. "The Theory of Hedging and Speculation in Commodity Futures Markets." *Review of Economic Studies*, vol. 27, no. 3 (October):139–151.

Kolb, Robert W. 1982. *Interest Rate Futures: A Comprehensive Introduction*. Richmond, VA: R.F. Dame.

———. 1985. *Understanding Futures Markets*. Glenview, IL: Scott Foresman Trade.

Kolb, Robert W., and Gerald D. Gay, eds. 1982. *Interest Rate Futures: Concepts and Issues*. Richmond, VA: R.F. Dame.

Kolb, Robert W., Gerald D. Gay, and William C. Hunter. 1985. "Liquidity Requirements for Financial Futures Hedges." *Financial Analysts Journal*, vol. 41, no. 3 (May/June):60–68.

Powers, Mark J. 1984. *Inside the Financial Futures Markets*. 2nd ed. Hoboken, NJ: John Wiley & Sons.

Schwarz, Edward W., Joanne M. Hill, and Thomas Schneeweis. 1986. *Financial Futures: Fundamentals, Strategies, and Applications*. Homewood, IL: Business One Irwin.

Sharpe, William F. 1985. *Investments*. 3rd ed. Boston: Prentice-Hall.

Siegel, Daniel R., and Diane F. Siegel. 1990. *Futures Markets*. Fort Worth, TX: Dryden Press.

## General References on Hedging

Ahadi, Hamid Z., Peter A. Sharp, and Carl H. Walther. 1986. "The Effectiveness of Futures and Options in Hedging Currency Risk." In *Advances in Futures and Options Research*, 1, Part B. Edited by Frank Fabozzi. Oxford, United Kingdom: JAI Press.

Ederington, Louis H. 1979. "The Hedging Performance of the New Futures Market." *Journal of Finance*, vol. 34, no. 1 (March):157–170.

Figlewski, Stephen. 1984. "Hedging Performance and Basis Risk in Stock Index Futures." *Journal of Finance*, vol. 39, no. 3 (July):657–669.

———. 1986. *Hedging with Financial Futures for Institutional Investors*. Pensacola, FL: Ballinger Publishing Company.

Gay, Gerald D., Robert W. Kolb, and Raymond Chiang. 1983. "Interest Rate Hedging: An Empirical Test of Alternative Strategies." *Journal of Financial Research*, vol. 6, no. 3 (Fall):187–197.

Hill, Joanne, and Thomas Schneeweis. 1981. "A Note on the Hedging Effectiveness of Foreign Currency Futures." *Journal of Futures Markets*, vol. 1, no. 4 (Winter):659–664.

Kolb, Robert W., and Raymond Chiang. 1981. "Improving Hedging Performance Using Interest Rate Futures." *Financial Management*, vol. 10, no. 4 (Fall):72–79.

Kolb, Robert W., and Gerald D. Gay, eds. 1982. "Risk Reduction Potential of Financial Futures for Corporate Bond Positions." In *Interest Rate Futures: Contracts and Issues*. Richmond, VA: R.F. Dame.

**Empirical Research on Forward and Futures Prices**

Cornell, B., and M. Reinganum. 1981. "Forward and Futures Prices: Evidence from Foreign Exchange Markets." *Journal of Finance*, vol. 36, no. 5 (December):1035–1045.

French, K. 1983. "A Comparison of Futures and Forward Prices." *Journal of Financial Economics*, vol. 12, no. 3 (November):311–342.

Park, H.Y., and A.H. Chen. 1985. "Differences between Futures and Forward Prices: A Further Investigation of Marking to Market Effects." *Journal of Futures Markets*, vol. 5, no. 1 (Spring):77–88.

Rendleman, R., and C. Carabini. 1979. "The Efficiency of the Treasury Bill Futures Markets." *Journal of Finance*, vol. 34, no. 4 (September):895–914.

**The Theoretical Relationship between Forward and Futures Prices**

Cox, J.C., J.E. Ingersoll, and S.A. Ross. 1981. "The Relation between Forward Prices and Futures Prices." *Journal of Financial Economics*, vol. 9, no. 4 (December):321–346.

Jarrow, R.A., and G.S. Oldfield. 1981. "Forward Contracts and Futures Contracts." *Journal of Financial Economics*, vol. 9, no. 4 (December):373–382.

Kane, E.J. 1980. "Market Incompleteness and Divergences between Forward and Futures Interest Rates." *Journal of Finance*, vol. 35, no. 2 (May):221–234.

Richard, S., and M. Sundaresan. 1981. "A Continuous Time Equilibrium Model of Forward Prices and Futures Prices in a Multi-Good Economy." *Journal of Financial Economics*, vol. 9, no. 4 (December): 347–371.

## General References on Options

Black, Fischer. 1975. "Fact and Fantasy in the Use of Options." *Financial Analysts Journal*, vol. 31, no. 4 (July/August):36–41, 61–72.

Black, Fischer, and Myron Scholes. 1973. "The Pricing of Options and Corporate Liabilities." *Journal of Political Economy*, vol. 81, no. 3 (May/June):637–659.

Bookstaber, Richard M. 1985. *The Complete Investment Book*. Glenview, IL: Scott Foresman Trade.

———. 1991. *Option Pricing and Investment Strategies*. Bloomington, IN: Probus Publishing Company.

Chance, D. 1989. *An Introduction to Options and Futures*. Fort Worth, TX: Dryden Press.

Choie, K., and F. Novomestky. 1989. "Replication of Long-Term with Short-Term Options." *Journal of Portfolio Management*, vol. 15, no. 2 (Winter):17–19.

Cox, John C., and Mark Rubinstein. 1985. *Options Markets*. Boston: Prentice-Hall.

Dengler, W.H., and H.P. Becker. 1984. "19 Option Strategies and When to Use Them." *Futures Magazine*, vol. 13 (June): http://media.futuresmag.com/futuresmag/historical/SiteCollectionDocuments/Guides_PDFs/19OptionsStrategies.pdf.

Figlewski, S., W. Silber, and M. Subrahmanyam, eds. 1990. *Financial Options: From Theory to Practice*. Salomon Brothers Center for the Study of Financial Institutions. Homewood, IL: Business One Irwin.

Hull, J. 1989. *Options, Futures, and Other Derivative Securities*. Prentice-Hall.

Jarrow, Robert, and Andrew Rudd. 1983. *Option Pricing*. Homewood, IL: Business One Irwin.

McMillan, Lawrence G. 1986. *Options as a Strategic Investment*. 2nd ed. New York: New York Institute of Finance.

Merton, Robert C. 1973a. "The Relationship between Put and Call Option Prices: Comment." *Journal of Finance*, vol. 28, no. 1 (March):183–184.

———. 1973b. "The Theory of Rational Option Pricing." *Bell Journal of Economics and Management Science*, vol. 4, no. 1 (Spring):141–183.

Ritchken, Peter. 1987. *Options: Theory, Strategy, and Applications*. Glenview, IL: Scott Foresman Trade.

Sharpe, William F. 1985. *Investments*. 3rd ed. Boston: Prentice-Hall.

Stoll, Hans R. 1969. "The Relationship between Put and Call Option Prices." *Journal of Finance*, vol. 24, no. 5 (December):319–332.

Yates, James W., and Robert W. Kopprasch. 1980. "Writing Covered Call Options: Profits and Risks." *Journal of Portfolio Management*, vol. 7, no. 1 (Fall):74–80.

## Black–Scholes Model and Extensions

Black, Fischer. 1988. "How to Use the Holes in Black–Scholes." *Journal of Applied Corporate Finance*, vol. 1, no. 4 (Winter):67–73.

Cox, John C., and Stephen A. Ross. 1976. "The Valuation of Options for Alternative Stochastic Processes." *Journal of Financial Economics*, vol. 3, nos. 1–2 (March):145–166.

Cox, John C., and Mark Rubinstein. 1983. "A Survey of Alternative Option Pricing Models." In *Option Pricing*. Edited by Menachem Brenner. Lexington, MA: Heath.

Cox, John C., Stephen A. Ross, and Mark Rubinstein. 1979. "Option Pricing: A Simplified Approach." *Journal of Financial Economics*, vol. 7, no. 3 (September):229–263.

Geske, R. 1979. "The Valuation of Compound Options." *Journal of Financial Economics*, vol. 7, no. 1 (March):63–81.

Hull, J., and A. White. 1987. "The Pricing of Options on Assets with Stochastic Volatilities." *Journal of Finance*, vol. 42, no. 2 (June):281–300.

Merton, Robert C. 1976. "Option Pricing When Underlying Stock Returns Are Discontinuous." *Journal of Financial Economics*, vol. 3, nos. 1–2 (January–March):125–144.

Rubinstein, M. 1983. "Displaced Diffusion Option Pricing." *Journal of Finance*, vol. 38, no. 1 (March):213–217.

Smith, Clifford W., Jr. 1976. "Option Pricing: A Review." *Journal of Financial Economics*, vol. 3, nos. 1–2 (January–March):3–51.

## Binomial Models

Boyle, P.P. 1988. "A Lattice Framework for Option Pricing with Two State Variables." *Journal of Financial and Quantitative Analysis*, vol. 23, no. 1 (March):1–12.

Cox, John C., Stephen A. Ross, and Mark Rubinstein. 1979. "Option Pricing: A Simplified Approach." *Journal of Financial Economics*, vol. 7, no. 3 (September):229–263.

Hsia, Chi-Cheng. 1983. "On Binomial Option Pricing." *Journal of Financial Research*, vol. 6, no. 1 (Spring):41–50.

Hull, J., and A. White. 1988. "The Use of the Control Variant Technique in Option Pricing." *Journal of Financial and Quantitative Analysis*, vol. 23, no. 3 (September):237–251.

## Option Volatilities

Beckers, S. 1981. "Standard Deviations in Option Prices as Predictors of Future Stock Price Variability." *Journal of Banking & Finance*, vol. 5, no. 3 (September):363–381.

Bookstaber, Richard M., and Steven Pomerantz. 1989. "An Information-Based Model of Market Volatility." *Financial Analysts Journal*, vol. 45, no. 6 (November/December):37–46.

Brenner, M., and M. Subrahmanyam. 1988. "A Simple Formula to Compute the Implied Standard Deviation." *Financial Analysts Journal*, vol. 44, no. 5 (September/October):80–83.

Chiras, D.P., and S. Manaster. 1978. "The Information Content of Option Prices and a Test of Market Efficiency." *Journal of Financial Economics*, vol. 6, nos. 2–3 (June–September):213–234.

Whaley, Robert E. 1982. "Valuation of American Call Options on Dividend-Paying Stocks: Empirical Tests." *Journal of Financial Economics*, vol. 10, no. 1 (March):29–58.

## Pricing American Options and Other Approaches

Barone-Adesi, G., and R.E. Whaley. 1987. "Efficient Analytic Approximation of American Option Values." *Journal of Finance*, vol. 42, no. 2 (June):301–320.

Boyle, P.P. 1977. "Options: A Monte Carlo Approach." *Journal of Financial Economics*, vol. 4, no. 3 (May):323–338.

Brennan, M.J., and E.S. Schwartz. 1977. "The Valuation of American Put Options." *Journal of Finance*, vol. 32, no. 2 (May):449–462.

———. 1978. "Finite Difference Methods and Jump Processes Arising in the Pricing of Contingent Claims: A Synthesis." *Journal of Financial and Quantitative Analysis*, vol. 13, no. 3 (September):461–474.

Courtadon, G. 1982. "A More Accurate Finite Difference Approximation for the Valuation of Options." *Journal of Financial and Quantitative Analysis*, vol. 17, no. 5 (December):697–705.

Geske, Robert. 1979. "A Note on an Analytic Formula for Unprotected American Call Options on Stocks with Known Dividends." *Journal of Financial Economics*, vol. 7, no. 4 (December):375–380.

———. 1981. "Comments on Whaley's Note." *Journal of Financial Economics*, vol. 9, no. 2 (June):213–215.

Geske, R., and H.E. Johnson. 1984. "The American Put Valued Analytically." *Journal of Finance*, vol. 39, no. 5 (December):1511–1524.

Hull, J., and A. White. 1990. "Valuing Derivative Securities Using the Explicit Finite Difference Method." *Journal of Financial and Quantitative Analysis*, vol. 25, no. 1 (March):87–100.

Johnson, H.E. 1983. "An Analytic Approximation to the American Put Price." *Journal of Financial and Quantitative Analysis*, vol. 18, no. 1 (March):141–148.

MacMillan, L.W. 1986. "Analytic Approximation for the American Put Option." In *Advances in Futures and Options Research*. Edited by Frank Fabozzi. Oxford, United Kingdom: JAI Press.

Roll, Richard. 1977. "An Analytic Valuation Formula for Unprotected American Call Options on Stocks with Known Dividends." *Journal of Financial Economics*, vol. 5, no. 2 (November):251–258.

Whaley, Robert E. 1981. "On the Valuation of American Call Options on Stocks with Known Dividends." *Journal of Financial Economics*, vol. 9, no. 2 (June):207–211.

———. 1982. "Valuation of American Call Options on Dividend Paying Stocks: Empirical Tests." *Journal of Financial Economics*, vol. 10, no. 1 (March):29–58.

## Options on Futures

Brenner, M., G. Courtadon, and M. Subrahmanyam. 1985. "Options on the Spot and Options on Futures." *Journal of Finance*, vol. 40, no. 5 (December):1303–1317.

Ramaswamy, K., and S.M. Sundaresan. 1985. "The Valuation of Options on Futures Contracts." *Journal of Finance*, vol. 40, no. 5 (December):1319–1340.

Shastri, Kuldeep, and Kishore Tandon. 1986. "Options on Futures Contracts: A Comparison of European and American Pricing Models." *Journal of Futures Markets*, vol. 6, no. 4 (Winter):593–618.

Whaley, Robert E. 1986. "Valuation of American Futures Options: Theory and Tests." *Journal of Finance*, vol. 41, no. 1 (March):127–150.

Wolf, A. 1982. "Fundamentals of Commodity Options on Futures." *Journal of Futures Markets*, vol. 2, no. 4 (Winter):391–408.

## Options on Currencies

Biger, Naham, and John Hull. 1983. "The Valuation of Currency Options." *Financial Management*, vol. 12, no. 1 (Spring):24–28.

Bodurtha, J.N., and G.R. Courtadon. 1987. "Tests of an American Option Pricing Model on the Foreign Currency Options Market." *Journal of Financial and Quantitative Analysis*, vol. 22, no. 2 (June):153–167.

Garman, M.B., and S.W. Kohlhagen. 1983. "Foreign Currency Option Values." *Journal of International Money and Finance*, vol. 2, no. 3 (December):231–237.

Grabbe, J.O. 1983. "The Pricing of Call and Put Options on Foreign Exchange." *Journal of International Money and Finance*, vol. 2, no. 3 (December):239–253.

## Options on Bonds

Black, Fischer, Emanuel Derman, and William Toy. 1990. "A One-Factor Model of Interest Rates and Its Application to Treasury Bond Options." *Financial Analysts Journal*, vol. 46, no. 1 (January/February):33–39.

Bookstaber, R., and J. McDonald. 1985. "A Generalized Option Valuation Model for the Pricing of Bond Options." *Review of Futures Markets*, vol. 4, no. 1:60–73.

Dattatreya, R., and F. Fabozzi. 1989. "A Simplified Model for Valuing Debt Options." *Journal of Portfolio Management*, vol. 15, no. 3 (Spring):64–72.

Macaulay, Frederick Robertson. 1910. *Money and Credit and the Price of Securities.* Boulder, CO: University of Colorado Press.

## Option Pricing

Black, Fischer, and Myron Scholes. 1972. "The Valuation of Option Contracts and a Test of Market Efficiency." *Journal of Finance*, vol. 27, no. 2 (May):399–418.

Bodurtha, J.N., and G.R. Courtadon. 1987. "Tests of an American Option Pricing Model on the Foreign Currency Options Market." *Journal of Financial and Quantitative Analysis*, vol. 22, no. 2 (June):153–168.

Chance, D.M. 1986. "Empirical Tests of the Pricing of Index Call Options." In *Advances in Futures and Options Research*. Edited by Frank Fabozzi. Oxford, United Kingdom: JAI Press.

Chiras, D., and S. Manaster. 1978. "The Information Content of Option Prices and a Test of Market Efficiency." *Journal of Financial Economics*, vol. 6, nos. 2–3 (September):213–234.

Galai, D. 1977. "Tests of Market Efficiency and the Chicago Board Options Exchange." *Journal of Business*, vol. 50, no. 2 (April):167–197.

Klemkosky, R.C., and B.G. Resnick. 1979. "Put–Call Parity and Market Efficiency." *Journal of Finance*, vol. 34, no. 5 (December):1141–1155.

MacBeth, J.D., and L.J. Merville. 1979. "An Empirical Examination of the Black–Scholes Call Option Pricing Model." *Journal of Finance*, vol. 34, no. 5 (December):1173–1186.

Shastri, K., and K. Tandon. 1986a. "An Empirical Test of a Valuation Model for American Options on Futures Contracts." *Journal of Financial and Quantitative Analysis*, vol. 21, no. 4 (December):377–392.

———. 1986b. "Valuation of Foreign Currency Options: Some Empirical Tests." *Journal of Financial and Quantitative Analysis*, vol. 21, no. 2 (June):145–160.

## Performance Evaluation of Options

Bookstaber, Richard M. 1986. "The Use of Options in Performance Structuring: Modeling Returns to Meet Investment Objectives." In *Controlling Interest Rate Risk: New Techniques and Applications for Money Management*. Edited by Robert B. Platt. Hoboken, NJ: John Wiley & Sons.

Bookstaber, Richard M., and Roger Clarke. 1985. "Problems in Evaluating the Performance of Portfolios with Options." *Financial Analysts Journal*, vol. 41, no. 1 (January/February):48–62.

Brooks, Robert, Haim Levy, and Jim Yoder. 1987. "Using Stochastic Dominance to Evaluate the Performance of Portfolios with Options." *Financial Analysts Journal*, vol. 43, no. 2 (March/April):79–82.

Clarke, Roger. 1987. "Stochastic Dominance Properties of Option Strategies." In *Advances in Futures and Options Research*, 2. Edited by Frank Fabozzi. Oxford, United Kingdom: JAI Press.

Slivka, Ronald T. 1980. "Risk and Return for Option Investment Strategies." *Financial Analysts Journal*, vol. 36, no. 5 (September/October):67–73.

# Glossary

**American option**. An option that can be exercised at any time during its life.

**Anticipatory hedge**. A long anticipatory hedge is initiated by buying futures contracts to protect against a rise in the price of an asset that will need to be purchased at a later date. A short anticipatory hedge is initiated by selling futures contracts to protect against the decline in price of an asset to be sold at a future date.

**Arbitrage**. A transaction based on the observation of the same or an equivalent asset selling at two different prices. The transaction involves buying the asset at the lower price and selling it at the higher price for a (theoretically) riskless profit.

**At the money**. As applied to an option for which the price of the underlying stock or futures equals the exercise price; an at-the-money option is neither in the money nor out of the money.

**Backwardation**. A condition in financial markets in which the forward or futures price is less than the expected future spot price.

**Bank discount rate**. A rate quoted on short-term non-interest-bearing money market securities. The rate represents the annualized percentage discount from face value at the time the security is purchased.

**Basis**. The price difference between the underlying asset and the futures contract, generally calculated as the cash price minus the futures price. For some futures, the basis may be calculated as the futures price minus the cash price so that the basis is represented as a positive number.

**Basis point**. A unit of measure equal to one one-hundredth of 1%. Equivalent numerical values are 0.01% and 0.0001. Basis points are sometimes verbally referred to as "beps" or written as the acronym "bps."

**Bear put spread**. An option strategy consisting of a long put and a short put at a lower strike price with the same maturity.

**Bear spread**. An option or futures spread designed to profit in a bear market.

**Beta**. A measure of the responsiveness of a security or portfolio to the market as a whole. The term is generally used in the context of equity securities.

**Binomial pricing model**. A model based on the assumption that at any point in time, the price of the underlying asset or futures contract can change to one of only two possible values.

**Black model**. A pricing model developed by Fischer Black for a European option on a forward contract.

**Black–Scholes model**. A pricing model developed by Fischer Black and Myron Scholes for a European option on an asset or security.

**Bond-equivalent yield**. The annualized yield on a short-term instrument adjusted so as to be comparable with the yield to maturity on coupon-bearing securities, which are usually compounded semiannually.

**Box spread**. An option strategy composed of a long bull call spread and a long bear put spread, with identical strike prices and time to expiration for each spread.

**Breakeven point**. The security price (or prices) at which a particular option strategy neither makes money nor loses money. It is generally calculated at the expiration date of the options involved in the strategy.

**Bull call spread**. An option strategy consisting of a long call and a short call at a higher exercise price, with the same maturity for both call options.

**Bull spread**. An option or futures spread designed to profit in a bull market.

**Butterfly spread**. An option transaction consisting of one long call at a particular exercise price, another otherwise identical long call at a higher exercise price, and two otherwise identical short calls at an exercise price between the other two.

**Calendar spread**. An option strategy consisting of the purchase of an option with a given expiration and the sale of an otherwise identical option with a different expiration. Also referred to as a *horizontal spread*.

**Call option**. An option that gives the holder the right to buy the underlying security at a specific price for a certain, fixed period of time.

**Carry** ("**cost of carry**"). A term associated with financing a commodity or cash security until it is sold or delivered. It can include storage, insurance, and assay expenses but usually refers only to the financing costs on repos (repurchase agreements), bank loans, or dealer loans used to purchase the security or asset.

**Cash-and-carry arbitrage**. A theoretically riskless transaction of a long position in the spot asset and a short position in the futures contract that is designed to be held until the futures expire. Such a transaction should earn the short-term riskless rate to eliminate any arbitrage profits.

**Cash settlement**. The feature of certain futures contracts or options that allows delivery or exercise to be conducted with an exchange of cash rather than the physical transfer of assets.

**Certificate of deposit (CD)**. A time deposit, usually with a bank or savings institution, that has a specific maturity, which is evidenced by a certificate.

**Cheapest to deliver (CTD)**. The bond or note that, if delivered on the Chicago Board of Trade's Treasury bond or note contract, provides the smallest difference between the invoice price and the cost of the bond or note.

**Clearinghouse**. An agency or corporation connected with an exchange through which all futures contracts are reconciled, settled, guaranteed, and later, either offset or fulfilled through delivery of the commodity. The clearinghouse is the mechanism through which financial settlement is made.

**Closing transaction**. A trade that reduces an investor's position. Closing buy transactions reduce short positions, and closing sell transactions reduce long positions.

**Collar**. An option strategy consisting of a long position in an underlying security and a short call and a long put with equal expiration dates, where the call has a higher strike price than the put.

**Commodity Futures Trading Commission (CFTC)**. An independent federal regulatory agency charged and empowered under the Commodity Futures Trading Commission Act of 1974 with regulation of futures trading and all futures options in all commodities. The CFTC's responsibilities include examining and approving all contracts before they may be traded on the exchange floor.

**Commodity pool**. An investment arrangement in which individuals combine their funds to trade futures contracts, with a large cash reserve set aside to meet margin calls.

**Commodity trading adviser (CTA)**. An individual who specializes in offering advice regarding the trading of futures contracts.

**Condor**. An option position consisting of two otherwise identical short call positions at separate strike prices and two long call positions at strike prices outside the strike prices of the two short positions.

**Contango**. A condition in financial markets in which the forward or futures price is greater than the expected future spot price.

**Continuously compounded return**. A rate of return between two points in time in which the asset price is assumed to grow or pay a return at a continuous rate.

**Convergence**. The narrowing of the basis as a futures contract approaches expiration.

**Conversion factor**. An adjustment factor applied to the settlement price of the Chicago Board of Trade's Treasury bond and note contracts that gives the holder of the short position a choice of several bonds or notes to deliver.

**Convexity**. A measure of the curvature of a bond's price line as interest rates change. Convexity is often used together with duration to approximate the change in the price of a bond as its yield to maturity changes.

**Coupon rate**. The rate of interest stated on a bond to be paid to the purchaser by the issuer of the bond. Interest payments on a bond are generally paid semiannually and are equal to the coupon rate multiplied by the face value, prorated for the payment period.

**Covered call**. A combination of a long position in an asset, futures contract, or currency and a short position in a call option on that asset.

**Covered interest arbitrage**. The purchase of an instrument denominated in a foreign currency and hedging of the resulting foreign exchange risk by selling the proceeds of the investment forward for dollars in the interbank market or going short in that currency in the futures market.

**Cross-hedge**. The hedging of cash market risk in one commodity or financial instrument by initiating a position in a futures contract for a different but related commodity or instrument. A cross-hedge is based on the premise that, although the two commodities or instruments are not the same, their prices generally move together.

**Current yield**. The return on an asset calculated by dividing the annual coupon payments by the current price of the asset. Accrued interest is typically omitted in the calculation.

**Daily settlement**. The process in a futures market in which the daily price changes are paid by the parties incurring losses to the parties making profits.

**Deferred contracts**. Futures contracts that call for delivery in the more distant months, as distinguished from nearby months.

**Delivery**. The tender and receipt of an actual financial instrument in settlement of a futures contract or the transfer of ownership or control of the underlying commodity or financial instrument under terms established by the exchange. The possibility that delivery can occur causes cash and futures prices to converge.

**Delivery factor**. See Conversion factor.

**Delivery month**. A calendar month during which delivery against a futures contract can be made.

**Delta**. The ratio of the change in an option's price to a given change in the underlying asset or futures price.

**Delta/gamma neutral**. A hedge position constructed from a combination of options, futures, and/or the underlying security that has both a net delta and a net gamma of zero for the combined position.

**Delta neutral**. A hedge position constructed from a combination of options, futures, and/or the underlying security that has a net delta of zero for the combined position.

**Dividend yield**. The ratio of the dividend to the stock price.

**Duration**. A measure of the size and timing of a bond's cash flows. Duration reflects the weighted average maturity of the bond and indicates the sensitivity of the bond's price to a change in its yield to maturity.

**DV01**. Dollar value impact of a 1 bp change in the yield of a fixed-income security or derivative. DV01 is closely related to the concept of duration.

**Dynamic hedge**. An investment strategy in which an asset is hedged by selling futures in such a manner that the position is adjusted frequently and simulates the price movement of an option strategy.

**Dynamic option replication**. The replication of the payoff of an option that is created by shifting funds appropriately between a risky asset and cash as the risky asset's price changes.

**Early exercise**. The exercise of an American option before its expiration date.

**Effective annual rate**. The annual rate of return of an investment if compounding occurred annually. The calculation of the effective annual rate allows for comparison of investments with different compounding frequencies.

**Eurodollar.** A dollar deposited in a European bank or a European branch of an American bank.

**European option.** An option that can be exercised only as it expires.

**Exercise.** To invoke the right granted under the terms of the option's contract to purchase or sell the underlying security. Call option holders exercise to buy the underlying security; put option holders exercise to sell the underlying security.

**Exercise price.** The price at which an option permits its owner to buy or sell the underlying security, futures, or currency.

**Expiration date.** The date after which an option or futures contract is no longer effective.

**Fair value.** The value of an option or futures contract as determined by an arbitrage relationship.

**Foreign exchange rate.** The rate at which a given amount of one currency converts to another currency.

**Forward contract.** A transaction in which two parties agree to the purchase or sale of a commodity at some future time. In contrast to futures contracts, the terms of forward contracts are often not standardized and the forward contract is not transferable or tradable to another party. Settlement of the gains and losses on forward contracts is usually not done on a daily basis as with futures contracts.

**Forward foreign exchange rate.** The rate associated with the purchase or sale of one currency for another currency on a specific deferred delivery date.

**Forward interest rate.** The rate implied by the relationship between spot rates of different maturities.

**Futures contract.** A standardized agreement between a buyer and a seller to purchase an asset or currency at a later date at a fixed price. In contrast to a forward contract, the futures contract trades on a futures exchange and is subject to a daily settlement procedure of gains and losses.

**Futures market.** A market in which contracts for the future delivery of commodities or financial instruments are traded. The term can refer to a specific exchange or the market in general.

**Futures option.** An option on a futures contract.

**Gamma.** The ratio of the change in the option's delta for a given change in the underlying asset or futures price.

**Hedge**. A transaction in which an investor seeks to protect a current position or anticipated position in one market (say, the spot market) by using an opposite position in another (say, the option or futures market).

**Hedge ratio**. The ratio of options or futures to a spot position (or vice versa) that achieves an objective, such as minimizing or reducing risk.

**Historical volatility**. The standard deviation of return on a security, futures, or currency obtained by estimating it from historical data over a recent time period.

**Horizontal spread**. See Calendar spread.

**Implied repo (repurchase agreement) rate**. The cost of financing a cash-and-carry transaction that is implied by the relationship between the spot and futures price.

**Implied volatility**. The standard deviation of return on the underlying security obtained when the market price of an option equals the price obtained when using an option-pricing model.

**Initial margin**. The amount each participant in the futures market must deposit to the participant's margin account at the time a buy or sell order is placed to open a position.

**Interest rate parity**. The relationship between the spot and forward foreign exchange rates and the interest rates of two currencies.

**In the money**. A call (put) option in which the price of the asset, futures, or foreign exchange rate exceeds (is less than) the exercise price.

**Intrinsic value**. For a call (put) option, the greater of zero or the difference between the security (exercise) price and the exercise (security) price.

**Inventory hedge**. A long inventory hedge is initiated by purchasing futures contracts to protect against a rise in the price of an asset held in a short position. A short inventory hedge is initiated by selling futures contracts to protect against a fall in the price of an asset currently held in a long position.

**Kappa**. See Vega.

**Last trading day**. The final day under exchange rules when trading may occur in a given contract month. Contracts outstanding at the end of the last trading day must be settled by delivery of the underlying commodity or securities or by cash settlement.

**Leverage**. The ability to control a large dollar amount of a commodity or cash instrument with a comparatively small amount of capital by using borrowed funds.

**LIBOR (London Interbank Offered Rate)**. The average interest rate with which London banks borrow money from each other; it is quoted for various currencies and various time frames. For example, the one-month U.S. dollar LIBOR is the average rate for borrowing or lending dollars for one month among London banks.

**Limit move**. An occurrence in which the futures price hits the upper or lower daily price limit set by the exchange.

**Long**. As an adjective, the term refers to a trader who has purchased an option or futures contract or the cash commodity or financial instrument and has not yet offset that position (e.g., "the buyer of a futures contract has a long position"). As an adverb, the term means the action of a trader taking a position in which the trader has bought option or futures contracts (or a cash commodity) without taking the offsetting action (e.g., "the buyer went long the futures contract").

**Macaulay duration**. The present value weighted time to maturity of the cash flows of a fixed-income security with fixed payments.

**Maintenance margin**. A sum, usually smaller than the initial margin, that must be maintained on deposit while a position is outstanding. When an account drops below the maintenance level, the broker issues a margin call requesting that enough money be added to bring the account back up to the initial margin level.

**Margin**. Money deposited by both buyers and sellers of futures contracts to ensure performance of the terms of the contract.

**Mark to market**. See Daily settlement.

**Maturity**. The time in the future when financial contracts are due or expire.

**Maximum price fluctuation**. See Limit move.

**Mean–variance comparison**. A comparison of risk and return for an asset that uses the mean and variance of returns. Risk–return charts often use standard deviation, the square root of variance.

**Minimum price fluctuation**. The smallest allowable increment of price movement in a given contract. It is also referred to as a *minimum tick*.

**Minimum-variance hedge ratio**. The ratio of futures contracts for a given spot position that minimizes the variance of the profit from the hedge.

**Modified duration**. A duration measure scaled by dividing the Macaulay duration by 1 plus the interest rate for the period of compounding. Modified duration measures the impact of a change in yield, in contrast to the original Macaulay duration, which measures the impact of a percentage change in yield. Macaulay duration is calculated by the average time to maturity of a security's cash flows, weighted by their present values.

**Money market rate**. The interest rate paid on money market instruments, such as certificates of deposit. The rate is a simple interest rate usually based on a 360-day year for the term of the deposit.

**Naked position**. An isolated long or short position in the cash or futures market that is not hedged, spread, or part of an arbitrage.

**Nearby contract**. The futures contract month trading for the most immediate delivery, as distinguished from distant or deferred months.

**Negative carry**. The net cost incurred when the cost of financing is greater than the yield on the asset being carried.

**Net cost of carry (net carry)**. The net cost of financing, which is equal to the cost of financing minus the yield on the asset being carried.

**Offsetting order**. A futures or option transaction that closes out a previously established long or short position.

**Open contract or position**. A contract that has been initiated but has not yet been liquidated or offset by subsequent sale or purchase or by going through the delivery process.

**Open interest**. The number of futures or option contracts that have been established but not yet offset or exercised.

**Open outcry**. The auction system used in the trading pits on the floor of the futures exchange. All bids and offers are made openly and loudly by public and competitive outcry and hand signals in such manner as to be available to all members in the trading pit at the same time.

**Option**. A contract that gives the holder the right, or choice, to buy or sell an asset for a fixed price on or before a specified date in the future.

**Option clearing corporation**. The issuer of all listed option contracts trading on national option exchanges.

**Option replication**. Techniques used to replicate the payoff of an option, including dynamic hedging, synthetic options, and a basket of other options.

**Option-sensitivity measure**. The change in option price or characteristics attributable to change in the price of the underlying security, interest rates, volatility, or time to expiration. See Delta, Gamma, Rho, Vega, and Theta.

**Out of the money**. A call (put) option in which the price of the asset, currency, or futures contract is less (greater) than the exercise price.

**Overvalued**. A condition in which a security, option, or futures is priced at more than its fair value.

**Payoff**. The amount of money received from a transaction at the end of the holding period.

**Payoff matrix**. See Value matrix.

**Payoff profile**. A graph of an option strategy payoff plotted with respect to the ending security price.

**Payout protection**. The downward adjustment of the exercise price of an option following a cash distribution from a security (e.g., ex-dividend price decline on stocks).

**Pit**. A location on the floor of a futures exchange designated for trading a specific contract or commodity.

**Portfolio insurance**. An investment strategy that uses combinations of securities, options, or futures and is designed to provide a minimum or floor value of the portfolio at a future date. It is equivalent to the payoff of a protective put on the portfolio.

**Position limit**. The maximum number of contracts that can be held as specified in federal regulations.

**Positive carry**. The net gain earned over time when the cost of financing is less than the yield on the asset being financed.

**Protective put**. An investment strategy involving the use of a long position in a put and an asset to provide a minimum selling price for the asset.

**Pure-discount bond**. A bond, such as a Treasury bill, that pays no coupon and sells at a discount from face or par value.

**Put–call futures parity**. The relationship among the prices of puts, calls, and futures on a security, commodity, or currency.

**Put–call parity**. The relationship between the prices of puts, calls, and the underlying security, commodity, or currency.

**Put option**. An option granting the holder the right to sell the underlying security or currency at a certain price for a specified period of time.

**Ratio spread**. An option strategy in which the ratio of long to short positions is different from 1.0.

**Repo**. See Repurchase agreement.

**Repurchase agreement**. A securities transaction in which an investor sells a security and promises to purchase it back in a specified number of days at a higher price reflecting the prevailing interest rate.

**Reverse repo agreement.** A securities transaction in which an investor buys a security with the promise to sell it back in a specified number of days at a lower price reflecting the prevailing interest rate and yield on the security.

**Rho**. The ratio of the change in an option price to a change in interest rates.

**Riskless asset**. A theoretical asset with a nominal return that is known with certainty. The return on a short-term Treasury bill is often used as a proxy for the riskless rate.

**Risk premium**. The additional return a risk-averse investor expects for assuming risk. The risk premium is often measured as the difference in expected return between the risky asset and a riskless asset, such as a Treasury bill.

**Rolling**. An action in which the investor closes current option or futures positions and opens other options or futures with different strike prices or maturities on the same underlying security.

**Securities and Exchange Commission (SEC)**. The U.S. federal agency responsible for regulating the securities and option markets.

**Settlement price**. The price established by a clearinghouse at the close of the trading session as the official price to be used in determining net gains or losses, margin requirements, and the next day's price limits. The term *settlement price* is also often used as an approximate equivalent to the term *closing price*.

**Sharpe ratio**. The ratio of an investment's risk premium (expected return above the riskless rate) to its volatility as measured by the standard deviation of returns.

**Short**. As an adjective, the term is applied to a trader who has sold option or futures contracts or the cash commodity and has not yet offset that position (e.g., "the seller of a futures contract has a short position"). As a verb, the term means the action of a trader taking a position in which he has sold option or futures contracts or made a forward contract for sale of the cash commodity or instrument (e.g., "he shorted the futures contract").

**Short straddle.** An option transaction that involves a short position in a put and a call with the same exercise price and expiration.

**Simple interest rate.** The interest rate used to calculate the interest payment for a specific period of time prorated for the portion of a year the maturity represents.

**Spot.** The characteristic of being available for immediate (or nearly immediate) delivery. An outgrowth of the phrase *on the spot*, spot usually refers to a cash market price for stocks or physical commodities available for immediate delivery.

**Spot price.** The price of an asset on the spot market.

**Spread.** An option or futures transaction consisting of a long position in one contract and a short position in another, similar contract.

**Stack hedge.** A hedge constructed by using nearby contracts with the intent to roll them over to deferred contracts when the hedge must be extended in time.

**Standard deviation.** A measure of the dispersion of a random variable around its mean. Standard deviation is the square root of the variance.

**Stock index.** An average of stock prices designed to measure the performance of a portfolio of stocks selected on the basis of the defined characteristics of the index.

**Stock index futures.** A futures contract on any underlying stock index.

**Straddle.** An option transaction that involves a long position in a put and a call with the same exercise price and expiration.

**Strangle.** An option transaction that involves a long position in a call and a put with the same expiration and for which the strike price of the call exceeds that of the put.

**Strike price.** See Exercise price.

**Strip hedge.** A hedge constructed by using contracts of varied maturities that match the timing of the exposures to be hedged.

**Synthetic call.** A combination of a long put option and a long asset, futures, or currency that replicates the behavior of a call option.

**Synthetic cash.** A combination of a long asset, a short call option, and a long put option that replicates the return on a riskless asset.

**Synthetic futures.** A combination of a long call option and a short put option that replicates the behavior of a long futures contract.

**Synthetic put.** A combination of a long call option and a short asset, currency, or futures that replicates the behavior of a put option.

**Term structure of interest rates.** The relationship between interest rates and maturities of zero-coupon bonds.

**Theta.** The ratio of the change of an option price to a change in expiration date.

**Time value.** The difference between an option's price and its intrinsic value.

**Time value decay.** The erosion of an option's time value as expiration approaches.

**Treasury bill.** Short-term pure-discount bond issued by the U.S. government with an original maturity of 91, 182, or 365 days.

**Treasury bond.** A coupon-bearing bond issued by the U. S. government with an original maturity of at least 10 years.

**Treasury note.** A coupon-bearing bond issued by the U.S. government with an original maturity of 1–10 years.

**Treynor ratio.** The ratio of an investment's risk premium to its beta, in contrast to the Sharpe ratio, which uses standard deviation instead of beta.

**Unbiased.** The characteristic of a forecast in which the prediction equals the actual outcome, on average, of a large number of predictions.

**Undervalued.** A condition in which a security, option, or futures contract is priced at less than its fair value.

**Underlying security.** The security that an investor has the right to buy or sell via the terms of the listed option or futures contract.

**Value matrix.** A matrix of values to show the payoff of an option strategy above and below the relevant exercise prices of the options used. Also called a payoff matrix.

**Variance.** A measure of the dispersion of a random variable around its mean; it is equal to the square of the standard deviation.

**Variation margin.** Money added to or subtracted from a futures account that reflects profits or losses accruing from the daily settlement.

**Variation margin call.** A demand for money issued by a brokerage house to a customer to bring the equity in an account back up to the margin level.

**Vega**. The ratio of a change in an option price to a change in the volatility of the underlying security. Sometimes referred to as *kappa*.

**Volatility**. A measure of the amount by which an underlying security is expected to fluctuate in a given period of time. Volatility is generally measured by the annualized standard deviation of percentage price changes in the security.

**Write**. To sell an option. The investor who sells is the *writer*.

**Yield curve**. A chart in which yield to maturity is plotted on the vertical axis and the maturity of a fixed-income security is plotted on the horizontal axis. It is similar to a term structure curve.

**Yield to maturity**. The internal rate of return of a debt instrument held to maturity. Capital gains or losses are considered as well as coupon payments. Semiannual compounding is typically assumed for bonds in the United States.

**Zero-coupon bond**. See Pure-discount bond.